FAITH U

Dedication

The purpose of a courageous, active faith is, as Elijah said, "So that these people will *know* that YOU, O LORD, ARE GOD, AND THAT *YOU* ARE TURNING THEIR HEARTS BACK AGAIN"

1 Kings 18:37

I thank my wonderful wife, Lilian, sons Philip (now assisting me on our team) and Paul, and my marvellous mother, Mrs Grace Banks, for the push and inspiration to seek THE DIVINE WORD, and to abide in such Faith.

FAITH UNLIMITED

Melvin Banks
with Simon Fox

Marshall Pickering
An Imprint of HarperCollins*Publishers*

First published in Great Britain in 1991 by Marshall Pickering

Marshall Pickering is an imprint of
HarperCollinsReligious
part of HarperCollins Publishers
77–85 Fulham Palace Road, London W6 8JB

Typeset by Medcalf Type Ltd, Bicester, Oxon
Printed and bound in Great Britain by
HarperCollins Manufacturing, Glasgow

Contents

Contents

Contents

Acknowledgements

Grateful thanks to all my staff and team, especially to our excellent typist, Mrs Angela Minto, and to the pastors and fellow ministers of the many churches with which I labour in bringing in the Gospel net full of fish day by day, week by week all the year through.

Special thanks to the ministers of the IGO (International Gospel Outreach) with whom I have so much rich friendship, David Greenow and Bob Searle in particular, and scores of others.

Also to ministers of Assemblies of God in the UK, and especially in France, the Netherlands, Belgium and Germany.

Not forgetting Noel and Kathy Klemenski, pastors of the thriving Revival Baptist Church, Kimberley, Nottingham, who give us so much personal encouragement, and Bob Fish of Manchester.

PART I
THE TRUTH OF
THE GOSPEL

1. The World's Greatest Theme

This book is all about what I like to call Christian faith themes. By that I mean the many wonderful facets of the faith which has been "handed down to the saints". However, the most glorious theme of that faith is the Lord Jesus Christ Himself. He is the very central theme of the living Gospel message for our day.

About forty years ago, when the Rev George Gunn was the minister at Juniper Green in Edinburgh, he was invited to a dinner at which the guest of honour was Winston Churchill. As these two men talked Churchill asked Gunn, "How many come to your church on a Sunday?"

"About three hundred," Gunn replied.

"What, every Sunday?" said the astonished Churchill. He pondered for a minute or two and them exclaimed, "We politicians couldn't do that. It must be your theme!"

We do indeed have a glorious Theme and message to proclaim. This desperate world needs to hear it. What an authority there is in the Christian prophetic voice, but how sad it is when that voice is silent.

The Apostle Paul was so thrilled by Christ, the great Theme of the Gospel, that years after he had set out on the long road of proclamation he was able to write, "I have not hesitated to proclaim to you the *whole* will of God" (Acts 20:27). The Greek word which is translated as "hesitated" here is *hupostellein*, which means "to pull down the sail". So Paul is saying, "I have not pulled down the sail – I have kept the flag flying. I have told the whole story. I have not cut corners, I have not changed the message to suit my hearers or the cultures in which I have preached. Regardless of whether it would offend or please them, I have told them the entire truth."

Tozer prophesied that compromise would be "the churches' greatest problem at the latter half of the twentieth century". We cannot and we must not change the glorious Theme of which God has given us charge. Our message must be the whole counsel of God. We must proclaim that Christ, God's incarnate Son, visited this planet, taught, healed, died, conquered death and rose again. We must declare that He lives, that He is the unchanging One!

One dark night in the North Sea an admiral, while on the bridge of his battleship, noticed with alarm that a light was approaching his vessel. He sent an urgent message out to it: "Change your direction by two degrees to the south – we are on a collision course!" Back came a reply: "Change your direction by two degrees to the north – we are on a collision course!" Amazed by this response, the admiral sent out another message: "I am an admiral – I order you to change your direction by two degrees to the south!" This was the reply: "I am an able seaman – please change your direction by two degrees to the north!" Absolutely exasperated by this flouting of his authority, the admiral sent this final message: "I am in command of a battleship – change your direction!" But back came the response: "I am in charge of a lighthouse! I cannot change course – you can!" Of course, the admiral then promptly did as the lighthouse keeper asked. The Word of God is like that lighthouse. Its message is changeless. We are heading for trouble if we try to change it.

There was no official ceremony when the first stone of the new Saint Paul's Cathedral was laid in 1675, but something occurred which greatly impressed the onlookers. Stones from the old cathedral, which had been burned down in the Great Fire of London in 1666, lay in a pile on the site. One of them was to be used as the first stone of the new building. Sir Christopher Wren, the architect, told one of the workmen to bring one of the stones from the pile. As he laid it in place the bystanders noticed that it happened to have carved on it the Latin word *resurgam*, which means, "I shall rise again". Wren felt that this was a sign that Christ's resurrection was the foundation upon which he must build his cathedral. Christ's dying and rising again is the mighty theme and message upon which we Christians must base everything that we do. It is the only true foundation for living in any age or culture. It is a changeless message. It is the world's greatest theme.

2. Someone Big Has Died

Some years ago a large number of Christian ministers gathered at a certain town to attend a conference. Some of the townsfolk were puzzled by this influx of visitors. "I can only assume," said one shopkeeper, "that someone big has died." In a sense he was quite right – that was exactly why the ministers were meeting together. For without the death of Christ there would be no Church, and for Christians there would be no faith, no peace, no life, no joy and no hope. Yes, Someone big has died to make life worthwhile:

> Because the sinless Saviour died,
> My sinful soul is counted free;
> For God, the Just, is satisfied
> To look on Him – and pardon me.

Jesus came into the world to die on the Cross for our sake. He, the sinless Christ, bore our sins for us so that we might be made righteous through Him. He did a glorious, astounding work on Calvary, giving us a Gospel of power and of mighty grace. He paid a great price so that we might belong to Him.

So the Cross of Christ is the very heart of the

Christian message. Michael Green has rightly declared that "The Cross is the core of the Gospel." John Stott has said, "No doctrine can be called truly Christian that is not centred on the Cross."

Very many years ago a wealthy young man was strolling around the city of Dusseldorf in Germany. In order to pass the time he went into the art gallery. He was deeply impressed by a picture of the Crucifixion painted by Steiner. The artist had begun to paint this masterpiece with little religious fervour, but he had finished it in a blaze of true devotion. Below it he had printed the words:

> All this I did for thee.
> What hast thou done for Me?

The young aristocrat was deeply challenged by the painting and its inscription, and he left the gallery a changed man. His name was Count Zinzendorf, and in the years ahead he was to found the Moravian Church and carry out a mighty missionary work for God. It was the challenge and appeal of the crucified Christ which brought about this great transformation in his heart.

The life of the believer and of the Church is by, through and on the blood of Christ. It is the very foundation of our faith. That blood, shed on the Cross, cleanses us from our sin. The Letter to the Hebrews tells us that "Jesus . . . suffered outside the city gate to make the people holy through his own blood" (13:12). I remember a preacher saying some years ago, "Calvary is the doorway to heaven and the barrier to hell." In the bloodstream of Calvary there is pardon, peace and tranquillity; in the bloodstream of Calvary there is omnipotence, forgiveness and a new beginning for man. None of us can afford to ignore that bloodstream. Those who despise the blood of Jesus cannot be washed clean in it!

An African young man was one day cutting down pampass grass with a machete knife. Unfortunately the knife slipped from his hand and cut off the back of one of his heels. There was a little mission hospital a mile or so away, so he staggered through the bush towards it, bleeding profusely. Finally he reached the hospital and collapsed upon its steps. The staff rushed out to help him. They quickly gave him a blood transfusion and so saved his life.

Not long after he had been put in a bed to recover his mother arrived, asking to see him. The staff were amazed. How could she have known that he had had an accident and that he had come to the hospital? She replied, "I followed the trail of blood, and it brought me here." There is significance in this story for us Christians, for we have been brought to our heavenly Father by the blood of His Son.

God sent Jesus to die on the Cross because of His great love for us. As Harrington Evans has said, "When God gave His son He gave an infinite proof of infinite love." This hymn speaks about that love:

> I sometimes think about the Cross,
> And shut my eyes and try to see
> The cruel nails and crown of thorns
> And Jesus crucified for me.
>
> But even could I see Him die,
> I could but see a little part

Of that great love which, like a fire,
Is always burning in His heart.

The author Elie Weisel records that while he was
at Auschwitz he and thousands of other prisoners
were forced to watch as the guards tortured and
hanged a young boy. Just before the hanging he
heard someone behind him whisper, "Where is God?
Where is He?" It took the boy half an hour to die.
Then the prisoners were made to walk past the dead
boy and look him full in the face. Behind him Elie
heard the same voice ask, "Where is God now?" He
writes that he then heard a voice within him answer,
"Where is He? Here He is – hanging here on the
gallows."

A Ukrainian lady who had attended one of my
meetings said to me, "The young women in your
services do not wear a cross. If they are Christians
they must wear a cross!" I replied, "Those who are
the Lord's children have the Cross in their hearts,
not around their necks!" How sad it is that people
have made the Cross into a mere emblem. Instead
it should be the very essence of our Christian living.
This is the challenge which Jesus has laid before us:
"If anyone would come after me, he must deny
himself and take up his cross daily and follow me"
(Luke 9:23).

3. The Galilean Conquers

When Bishop Mervyn Stockwood was once visiting Moscow his razor happened to break, so he had to go to a barber to get a shave. The lady barber noticed the pectoral cross which he was wearing and through an interpreter asked if he were a bishop. Answered in the affirmative, she kissed his cross, held up her razor (all covered with lather and hairs!) and shouted, "Christ is risen!" At once everyone else in the salon replied, "He is risen indeed!" (This was typical of Russian Orthodox Christians, who worship God with great fervour.) Later Stockwood wrote, "Poor old Communism – sixty years of atheism, and still the Galilean conquers!"

The great artist Tommasco Campanella urged his fellow painters to "Paint Christ not dead, but risen . . . paint Him the conqueror of death, the irresistible victor." Henry Liddon wrote, "No other spot on earth says so much to Christian faith as does the empty tomb of our Lord." Indeed, the Resurrection is part of the very heart of the Gospel. And yet many today do not believe that Christ was raised from the dead. Professor David Jenkins, Bishop of Durham, is by no means the first person to have doubts about the doctrine of the

Resurrection. He said on television a little while ago, "Sometimes I believe he was raised out of the tomb, sometimes I don't believe it!" He went on to dismiss the Resurrection as a "conjuring trick with bones". He is in the company of such renowned atheists as Renan, who claimed, "I would not believe Jesus rose even if I saw it." Some years ago, when Aneurin Bevan (the well-known Socialist leader who founded the National Health service in 1948) was attending his mother's funeral, he was asked if he believed in the resurrection of the body. He looked at the questioner silently for a moment and then replied, "My heart would like to believe it, but my mind won't let me." So many people have, like him, become stuck in their little worlds of unbelief.

Jesus told His disciples, "The Son of Man must suffer many things . . . and he must be killed and on the third day be raised to life" (Luke 9:22). He also said, "I lay down my life – only to take it up again. No-one takes it from me, but I lay it down of my own accord" (John 10:17-18). Paul wrote that Jesus Christ "was declared with power to be the Son of God by his resurrection from the dead" (Romans 1:4). He also wrote of the importance of the empty tomb: "If Christ has not been raised, your faith is futile; you are still in your sins" (1 Corinthians 15:17).

It is inconceivable that death could defeat the Living God. All the forces of hell tried to keep Jesus in the tomb, and yet they failed. Ever since His resurrection occurred they have been using slurs and doubts in an attempt to discredit it. They have also suggested all sorts of implausible theories about how

Christ's body escaped from the grave. But, as the great Abraham Lincoln declared, "The Resurrection is the best-proven fact of history."

The remarkable American writer Markham wrote a poem called *A Guard at the Sepulchre* which includes these lines:

> I saw your risen Christ for I am . . .
> One of the two who watched beside
> The sepulchre of Him who was crucified . . .
> Years I have wandered and carried my shame,
> For we who all the wonder might have told,
> Kept silent, for our mouths were stuffed with gold.

Are you silent about Christ's risen life? Does it fail to thrill you? Isn't Christ enough for you? Doesn't He satisfy you any longer? Have you lost the confidence to witness to others about Him? I pray for you what Paul prayed for his converts at Ephesus: "that the eyes of your heart may be enlightened in order that you may know . . . his incomparably great power for us who believe. That power is like the working of his mighty strength, which he exerted in Christ when he raised him from the dead" (Ephesians 1:18-20).

Thank God that Jesus burst out of the grave, scattered His enemies, leapt into Hades, set captives free, spoiled principalities and powers, gave gifts to men, made a conquering comeback and turned the tide in the universe, routing the devil and evil for ever!

4. The King Returns Home

When I was a boy I was involved with the Salvation Army, and I well remember how much importance the Salvationists used to attach to Ascension Day. They used to hold big rallies and parades to celebrate the fact that Jesus, having completed His mission on earth, had returned to the Glory Land above. Today Ascension Day is a largely forgotten occasion, except in the Church of England. However, Jesus' ascension to heaven is just as significant and exciting a fact now as it ever was, and we do well to think about it. Charles Wesley wrote:

> Hail the day that sees him rise,
> To his throne above the skies!
> Christ awhile to mortals given,
> Reascends to his native heaven.

Luke wrote of "the day he was taken up to heaven" (Acts 1:2). David wrote prophetically, "He ascended into the heights with captives in his train" (Psalm 68:18, NEB), or, as the Ways translation puts it, "He went up . . . and led captive a train of vanquished foes." It was the final seal on His resurrection − it was a *victorious exit*. It was also a *prelude to His glorious Second Coming*. As the angel said in Acts, "This same Jesus, who has been taken from you into heaven, will come back in the same way you have seen him go into heaven" (1:11).

Would it have been better if Jesus had not ascended? If He had stayed on earth, visible to all humanity, would they have been any more willing to accept Him as Lord and King? I doubt it. They would have tried to get rid of Him and crucify Him again and again.

In any case, because He has ascended and we have not actually seen Jesus, our faith in Him is of greater worth to God. Peter said, "Though you have not seen him, you love him; and even though you do not see him now, you believe in him and are filled with an inexpressible and glorious joy, for you are receiving the goal of your faith, the salvation of your souls" (1 Peter 1:8-9).

The hymn-writer J. Graves wrote:

> O Prince of Peace who once did rise
> In splendid triumph to the skies
> Before the rapt disciples' eyes . . .

W. E. Sangster commented, "The cloud that day hid *Him* from them, but it did not hide *them* from *Him*." Jesus has left us in a bodily sense, but He still watches over us. Scripture says, "the eyes of the Lord range throughout the earth" (2 Chronicles 16:9). Had Jesus not ascended, He would not be able to watch over us from heaven's vantage point, from which He can see everything.

Because He has gone to heaven, we can go there too. He ascended magnificently to open the door for all those who love and follow Him. He has left the door open so that we may receive from Him and one day go where He has gone. Henry Longfellow wrote:

> When Christ ascended
> Triumphantly from star to star,
> He left the gates of heaven ajar . . .

A great French astronomer was about to deliver a lecture to a gathering of notable dignitaries. In the preamble many fine compliments were paid to him and much was made of his outstanding scientific work. One eminent church leader said, "You have raised yourself to the stars." In reply to this the astronomer said, "It is not sufficient to have reached the stars. I mean to ascend higher. I mean one day to ascend to heaven itself, with the help of your prayers!" Yes, we believers will follow Jesus into heaven. He Himself prayed, "Father, I want those you have given me to be with me where I am" (John 17:24).

If we are believers we are one day going to see the King in all His beauty. We have seats booked on the glory train which will soar into the heavens, heading for the Shining City. That's why we must never forget Ascension Day!

5. God's Big Chance

Throughout the Bible man cries over his sin. Balaam said to the angel, "I have sinned . . . I will go back" (Numbers 22:34). King Saul said, "I have sinned. I violated the Lord's command" (1 Samuel 15:24). Job declared, "I have sinned, what shall I do?" (Job 7:20, AV). The prodigal son said, "Father, I have sinned against heaven and against you" (Luke 15:21).

The Bible tells us that man fell from his original innocent state into his present sinful condition. This is no fairy story. There really was an Adam and an Eve, and they really did choose evil, rebellion and sin rather than goodness, love, perfection and obedience. People have been making the very same choice ever since then! One writer has wittily remarked that "Newton saw an apple fall and discovered the law of gravity, but Eve made an apple fall and discovered the gravity of the Law!" As C. S. Lewis has said, "man is not just an imperfect creature – *he is a rebel*". Robbie Burns expressed this truth powerfully:

> My ancient but ignoble blood
> Has crept through scoundrels
> Since the Flood. . . .

An unbeliever once told the Welsh evangelist Seth Joshua, "I can't swallow this doctrine of original sin." Joshua replied, "You don't have to — it's inside you already!"

As a result of the invasion of our planet by sin man has become a stranger to his Maker. He lives according to the ways of the world and far away from the presence of God. The Bible tells us that people are radically depraved. Psalm 58 tells us, "from the womb they are wayward and speak lies" (verse 3). Solomon says, "The hearts of men . . . are full of evil and there is madness in their hearts while they live" (Ecclesiastes 9:3). Psalm 14 says, "there is no one who does good, not even one" (verse 3). Man is broken, hurt, blighted and without hope. Disraeli called man "an archangel slightly damaged", but he understated the case. Nearer the mark is the cynical Chinese proverb which says, "There are only two good men — one of them is dead, and the other is not yet born." John Knox declared, "In youth, in middle age . . . and now . . . I find nothing but corruption." Augustus Toplady confessed, "In my whole flesh naturally dwelleth no good thing." In reality man is at his wit's end, beyond human reformation, reclamation or rejuvenation. Man needs a miracle to save him.

Once a little boy fell from a high building. However, he landed on some soft grass and merely bruised his ankles badly. His mother was overwhelmed with relief when she found that he wasn't seriously hurt. She noticed that he didn't seem too upset by the experience and asked him, "Weren't you frightened as you fell all that way?"

"No, I wasn't," he replied, beaming, "because I said a prayer to God as I fell."

His mother was surprised by this and asked, "What did you pray?"

"I just said to God, 'This is your big chance, God!' And He took it!"

Indeed, in human history God took his big chance. He saw that man was fallen, impaired, ensnared, lost, sinful, undeserving, wayward, sad and forlorn. He took the opportunity, He showed that He cared, He gave man a way out. He answered man's anguished cries for an answer to his predicament. He sent His Son into the world. Jesus can set people free from the bondage of sin. Praise God that through Jesus Christ man can be restored, ransomed, reborn, remade and rehabilitated!

6. Jesus Paid the Price

When I was a youngster Friday was the day of the livestock market in my howm town of Chippenham in Wiltshire. I have vivid memories of those market days. I remember seeing pigs, sheep, cattle and hens being brought for sale from the outlying villages in rattling old lorries. There was the smell of straw everywhere, the happy chatter between friends, the changing of money, the handshakes when a deal was done. I recall the auctioneer – he had a jargon all of his own that only he and the farmers were acquainted with. He thundered away at a hundred words a minute like a verbal machine gun, seeking the highest price. When the price would go no higher he would bang his gavel on the hard, wooden counter in front of him. If the price was a good one there would be a wide grin on his face. At the end of the day boys like myself would get half a crown from old "peg-leg" Tom (he had been injured in the First World War and so had a wooden leg) for helping him get the cattle to the railway station. There they would be herded onto trucks, and would then be taken either to a new owner or to an abbatoir somewhere. Those market days in our little country town were wonderful. It was a different world to this mad modern society. It had a certain fellowship, and a lack of bustle and rush.

It is thought that the ancient Romans invented the idea of sale by auction. Indeed, the English word "auction" comes from the Latin *auctio*, meaning "increase". Spoils taken in war were usually sold in this way. The sale was called a *sub hasta* ("under the spear"). A spear stuck in the ground was the signal for likely purchasers to gather. In England in the eighteenth and nineteenth centuries goods were often sold "by the candle". A short piece of candle was lit by the auctioneer and bids could be made while it stayed alight. Today the goods are described or viewed, and then a call for offers is made. The auctioneer finally concludes the sale by banging down his gavel (this is known as "knocking down") and naming the highest bidder as the successful purchaser. Often a bidder will pay a high price to prevent a rival from gaining possession.

In the Old Testament prophecy of Hosea we read that the prophet's wife was unfaithful to him and was finally sold by her paramour at a slave market. The anguished Hosea yearned to have her back, bidded successfully for her and restored her, forgiven, to her former state as his wife. All this is a kind of parable illustrating the lengths to which God was prepared to go in order to win back His erring, faithless children, the Jewish nation.

What was true of a whole people then is also true of every person today. Jesus Himself was the purchase price at the Great Auction; with Jesus' life God has bought us back from sin and death. What great value God must place on each of us, to buy us with the life of His Son!

Private John Simpson was one of the stretcher bearers who during the Gallipoli campaign in the First World War regularly traversed Shrapnel Gully, the road between the beaches and the front line. The road was so named because it was ceaselessly bombarded by the Turkish army. Between them he and a donkey brought wounded men to the safety of a dressing station on one of the beaches. In twenty-four days this ordinary man, who scorned both rewards and personal safety, saved many lives – no one knows how many. Eventually a machine-gun bullet put an end to his heroism. His gravestone bears these words: "He gave his life that others might live." That was exactly what Jesus Christ did for us.

The Roman writer Seneca tells the story of how Cornelia, the wife of Sempronius Gracchus, silenced a somewhat overbearing and proud acquaintance. Cornelia was visited one afternoon by a woman who made a point of showing off her expensive jewels. Obviously she hoped to make Cornelia ashamed of her lack of ornaments, since she was simply but tastefully dressed. The woman went on and on about her jewels – about what they had cost, which ones she liked most and why she had chosen to wear those particular ones that day. The quiet, dignified and very gracious Cornelia contrived to detain her guest until her two small boys arrived home from school. She introduced them, saying pleasantly but very meaningfully, "These are my jewels!" This story has survived nearly twenty centuries and serves to remind us that people, even very young ones or seemingly unimportant ones, are worth much more than riches.

God loves you and I, and places inestimable value upon us. He has paid the highest possible price so that you and I might belong to Him. We are ransomed and redeemed; we are the children of the King. We have been adopted into the family of God, and we are heading with Jesus for our final, heavenly abode – the New Jerusalem.

7. Lost Sheep

A writer was on holiday in the Scottish Highlands. When out for a walk one day he saw a shepherd standing alone and still, apparently peering up into the sky. The writer asked him what he was looking at. The old shepherd turned to him and replied in a broad Highland accent, "Laddie, can ye not see those lost sheep away up there?" He pointed to a rocky crag high up on a nearby mountain. Straining his eyes, the writer could just make out some tiny white blobs at the edge of what appeared to be a sheer drop.

"Can't you get up there and rescue them?" he asked.

The shepherd fought back a tear, and gulping down a lump in his throat murmured, "Aye, we can get up there all right, but if the sheep hear the slightest noise they'll get frightened and run over the edge. . . . I'm afraid they're lost. . . . They're lost!"

The writer walked away, deeply moved by the old shepherd's distress.

At the Amsterdam Congress of Evangelism some years ago Henri Blocher declared that "The mission of Jesus cannot be defined without speaking of man as being *lost*." In his Word God has said, "My people have been lost sheep" (Jeremiah 50:6). But He has also said, "I myself will search for my sheep and look after them" (Ezekiel 34:11). Jesus said of Himself, "the Son of Man came to seek and to save what was lost" (Luke 19:10).

Most people have no idea that they are lost. They need Christ as their Saviour, Lord and Friend, but they do not know it. Many people are hard and apathetic and oblivious to the fact that they are on a downward journey to hell and damnation. God is calling them, all heaven awaits them, the Kingdom's door is ever open to them, but they continue to be wayward and lost.

Some years ago a very fierce blizzard swept across parts of North America. Many communities were cut off by heavy snowfalls. People started to become concerned about a cartain old man who lived alone in a mountain cabin. After the blizzard had been going on for several days a two-man Red Cross team made a gallant attempt to rescue him by helicopter. They landed a mile from the cabin and then struggled through the deep snowdrifts. Reaching the almost-buried cabin, they shovelled the snow away from the door and knocked on it. There was no reply. They began wondering if the old man might be ill or dead. But then the door opened.

"We're from the Red Cross," said one of the exhausted rescuers.

The tough, bearded old man looked puzzled and scratched his head. "Well," he drawled, "I ain't got nuthin' to give ya — but come on in and have a cup o' coffee. You sure look like you need it!"

The old man seemed unaware of the fact that he

was cut off from the outside world and in great danger. In a similar way, many people do not realise that they are lost and in a dangerous spiritual condition.

When I was in Hawaii some years ago I saw a marvellous statue of Christ. It was not beautiful, like a statue by an Italian artist; instead it was realistic and vivid. It depicted Jesus carrying a lamb. It looked peaceful and secure in His arms. But Jesus' face was strained, wet, haggard and tired. He had been out all night, searching in the cold, foggy mountains for the lost sheep. He had been prepared to suffer – even to die – in order to rescue His lost sheep.

Millions of people are at this moment lost – lost to Jesus, lost to heaven, lost to all that is noblest and best in this life. Finally they will be lost forever. They do not know the way to Jesus. Let us run to them with the message. We should not rest until they are safe in His arms. God asks, "Whom shall I send? And who will go for us?" (Isaiah 6:8). Who will go with the Gospel message to the lost people of the world? It is we who must respond to this call.

8. A Change of Heart

In Kenneth Grahame's *Wind in the Willows* we read of Badger's vain attempts to get Toad to repent of his sins, one of the worst of which is his habit of stealing cars and smashing them up! Badger pleads with Toad in the smoking room of Toad Hall. Finally Toad gives in and says, "Go on then – I will repent!" Badger then throws open the door of the room and proudly announces Toad's conversion to the crowd of waiting animals and assures them that he "will be the most converted animal there ever was!" Later Toad is interrogated by his amazed friends and is asked, "Did you really repent?" With a red face he replies, "I only did it to please Badger!"

To some people the word "repentance" suggests fanaticism, and they think of the strange man they sometimes see on Saturday afternoons in the High Street who carries a placard saying, *"Repent – the end of the world is at hand!"* Such behaviour may seem odd, but perhaps placards like that do stir people's consciences.

The New Testament Greek word which is translated as "repentance" is *metanoia*, which means "a change of mind". A word which is often used in connection with *metanoia* is *avontee*, which means "with regret and double sorrow". One Bible dictionary defines repentance as "regret that causes a complete change of action". Repentance is a deep change of heart. It is not a shallow emotion or a self-effacing act or an empty experience. It is the life-transforming act of turning to God. It breaks the captive sinner's chains and sets him free, and it causes heaven to sing!

I like the Bible story of the woman who touched the hem of Jesus' garment. When He challenged her about this she came to Him and told Him the whole truth about herself (see Mark 5:25-34). Now that is real repentance – telling God all about your life, giving it over to Him, changing your direction, sharing your life with Him, turning your sin unto Him once and for all. Repentance is real and deep and life-changing.

Spurgeon expressed the transforming quality of repentance in this little rhyme:

> Repentance is to leave
> The sins we loved before
> And show that we in earnest grieve
> By doing so no more.

A candidate for ordination was asked by the officiating archbishop to define repentance. He answered, "Repentance is to have a heart which is broken because of sin." The pontiff replied, "No it's not! Repentance is to have a heart that is *broken away from sin!*" Repentance is a rapid and complete break with sin.

One day my wife and I were travelling along a country road to get to a meeting. We had been on this road a number of times before, so we knew the way quite well. After a while my wife told me, "Melvin, you've missed the turning – you should have taken that road on the right which we passed a mile back."

"No," I replied, "I think we're still going in the right direction. We haven't got to our turning yet."

"But I'm sure we've missed our turning," persisted my wife.

I refused to heed her and continued driving in the same direction. However, soon after that we passed a church and a village which I had never seen before, and I wondered if my wife was right after all. Soon I stopped the car, sure by then that I was wrong. I turned the car around and drove back a few miles and found the turning which we had missed. I think this story provides a picture of repentance. Repentance is realising that you are on the wrong road, stopping, admitting that you are going the wrong way, turning around and setting out on the right road (that is, God's road).

No-one should think that he can afford to delay repentance. Fuller has said, "You cannot repent too soon, because you do not know how soon it will be too late." An old and wise Rabbi was once asked by a young man, "When should I repent?" He shrewdly replied, "The day before you die." The baffled man asked, "But how can I know when I will die?" "You don't know the day," said the Rabbi, "so you had better repent today!"

I personally knew the Pentecostal preacher John Nelson Parr and was often at his red-hot Gospel meetings. He used to say, "Repentance is to say goodbye to this world of sin, to the flesh and the devil. It's turning your back on the old ways, old life, old pals, old habits and turning your life Godward, Christward and heavenward. Do it now!"

There is far too little emphasis on repentance in the Church today. I was once warned that if I continued with my "heavy Gospel preaching" no-one would come to hear me any more. Well, I have continued to preach my repentance Gospel, because it is God's Word. Contrary to what was predicted by my critics, the numbers of people coming to hear me have increased rather than decreased. Even if they had decreased, I would still preach that same Gospel to my dying day, because it is the only true Gospel. May today's preachers, churches and people find, seek and preach repentance!

9. Getting on the Right Wavelength

Recently I was trying to tune in to a certain BBC radio broadcast which was going to include a prerecorded interview of myself. But try as I might, I couldn't find the programme. I discovered later that I had tried to find it on the wrong wavelength. And it's not only radios which can be tuned to the wrong wavelength – people can be too. Sometimes they fail to understand one another, and that's because they are either not communicating clearly or not listening attentively.

A new-born baby was being dedicated at a certain church. At the service the minister waxed eloquent about the life that lay ahead of the child whom he was holding in his arms. "Think of the future before him," he said. "He may become a leader of industry, a captain in the Navy, a clergyman like myself, or a gifted teacher on whom hundreds of boys may model themselves." Then, turning to the parents, he asked grandly, "What name do you give this child?" The embarassed father replied, "Amanda Jane . . ." The minister was on the wrong wavelength!

Fred and Daphne have been married for over fifty years. Like many husbands, Bill is given to reading out snippets from the newspapers, expecting his wife to be interested. Marion has perfected the art of the gentle reply. This enables her to keep Bill happy while scarcely interrupting her own thoughts. One day Bill's eyebrows went up as he read the morning paper. "It says here," he informed his wife, "that a man is run over in New York every half an hour!" "Goodness," replied Marion, "you'd think that by this time he'd have learned to look when he's crossing the road!" Bill nodded in agreement and went on reading. They weren't really listening to each other!

Many teachers say they find it difficult to communicate with their pupils. In some ways television doesn't help them in their task. A certain teacher had been telling her class of seven year-olds about the Middle East and had mentioned Damascus once or twice. She noticed that one girl wasn't paying attention. "Judith," she said severely, "can you tell me anything about Damascus?" "Yes, Miss," replied Judith with a confident smile. "It kills ninety-nine per cent of all known germs!"

Of course, to some extent we all fail in communication. No-one is completely immune. Many parents find it difficult to make their teenage children see things their way. Their children see adults as out of date and unable to understand them.

A few years ago many of the national newspapers carried headlines like "The Church has failed." This was the view of the Prime Minister of the time, who had rapped the knuckles of the ecclesiastical system for failing to communicate its message of faith, hope and morality to the nation. There was a good deal of truth in this criticism. The message of the Gospel is timeless and never out of date. It is always relevant, even to a rapidly changing society. It speaks to the need of every generation. However, so often those who present the message are out of touch with the society in which they live. They are simply not on the wavelength of the ordinary people around them. As a result people can't understand the Gospel message.

Today we Christians need to remember that if we communicate the Gospel in the right way, in terms which today's people can comprehend, then they will listen to us. The empty, hungry multitudes, both young and old, are waiting to hear the Gospel. In the power of the Spirit of God we must impart the Bible's message to today's world!

10. Is there Life after Death?

I have estimated that I have answered about a million questions in my lifetime! I'm always being asked questions – face-to-face, on the radio, on television, on the phone. My staff deal with some 20,000 letters annually, and they are full of questions. People want to know the truth about life and death, they want to know the answers to their needs. I would say that the question I have been asked most often in the thirty-seven years of my ministry is this one: "Is there life after death?" People want to know what, if anything, lies beyond the grave; they want to know where they will go when this life ends.

C. S. Lewis was so sure about the afterlife that he named his house "Shadowlands". This reminded him that his earthly life was only a shadow of the life that was to come.

Peter likened this present life to living in a tent (2 Peter 1:13). At death we fold up the tent and move on to a new camping site. I was on a campsite in my caravan recently. Some people stayed just for one night. I would see them arrive in the evening, and in the morning I would wake to find that they and all their belongings had vanished. Others would stay for days or even for weeks. Somehow this all reminded me of life.

There is a certain mystery surrounding death. C. S. Lewis' gravestone in Headington Cemetery reads, "Men must endure their going hence." It is something which we cannot fully understand but which we must all go through. And then there is the further mystery of the resurrection from the dead. Paul said, "Listen, I tell you a mystery: We will not all sleep, but we will all be changed – in a flash, in the twinkling of an eye, at the last trumpet. For the trumpet will sound, the dead will be raised imperishable, and we will be changed. For the perishable must clothe itself with the imperishable, and the mortal with immortality" (1 Corinthians 15:51-53).

Doctor Don Gray Barnhouse lost his wife, Lucy, and was left with three small children to care for alone. Shortly after her death he was taking the children somewhere in his car when a large lorry overtook them. For a few moments they were out of the sunlight, completely immersed in the shadow of the lorry. Barnhouse asked one his children, "Which would be better – that lorry running over us, or just its shadow runing over us?" "It's shadow running over us, of course," the child replied. "Well, something like that has happened to your Mum," Barnhouse explained. "She hasn't been run over by death, but just by the shadow of death." We Christians need not fear death. It cannot destroy us, even though its shadow must one day pass over us.

In Bunyan's *Pilgrim's Progress* Christian, crying, "O death, where is thy sting? O grave, where is thy victory?" is carried over the swirling waters of the river of death by angels, and as he reaches the other side trumpets sound for him in the Celestial City. Death holds no terror for the Christian.

It is interesting to read the last words of notable people who were ready to face death. John Knox said, "Die in Christ and the flesh need not fear death." Ausustus Toplady, writer of the famous hymn, "Rock of Ages", said, "I'm enjoying heaven already." Richard Baxter of Kidderminster said, "I have pain but I have peace." Alexander Lyte cried jubilantly, "Joy! . . . Joy! . . . Peace! . . ." Martin Luther said, "God is the Lord with whom we escape death."

If we are Christians we can have a bright, confident attitude to death. When Charles Kingsley lay dying his wife was also dangerously ill. From her bed in another room she sent a servant to him with this message: "It is cowardly to tremble before the mystery of that unknown next world." He sent a note back: "My dear, it is not darkness we are going to, for *God is light*, not loneliness. *Christ is with us*."

Recently I was preaching in Arnhem in Holland. While I was there I visited the famous Osterbeek Airborne Cemetery, which contains the graves of 1,700 British paratroopers. Most of them were very young men in their early twenties or even in their teens. I was very moved by these words on the gravestone of one nineteen year-old glider crewman:

He is not lost –
He has stepped into heaven's loveliest room
And has left the door ajar

His loving parents had put these words on the stone. They were words of assurance and hope, of trust in the Saviour's promises.

A young boy was asked to tell the biblical story of Enoch in his own words. He told it like this: "Enoch used to go on long walks with God. One day they walked further than usual and God said, 'Enoch, you're tired. Come into my house and rest.' So he did." What a lovely way to describe death!

A little girl whose baby sister had just died asked her mother where she had gone. "She's gone to be with Jesus," was the reply. A few days later the girl heard her mother say to someone, "I'm devastated about losing the baby." Later the girl asked her, "Mum, is a thing lost when you know where it is?" "No, of course not," replied her mother. "So why do you say the baby is lost when she's gone to be with Jesus?"

A small boy's grandmother had died. His mother wondered how to explain to him what had happened. Finally she told him, "I've got some sad news for you, Peter. We won't be seeing Granny any more." "Oh," he said, puzzled. "Why, Mummy?" "Because she's gone to live with God." "Crumbs!" exclaimed the boy. "How posh!"

In *The Wind in the Willows* Toad, on being released from prison, exclaims, "I'm free, and all the world is mine!" Heaven will be like that. It will be a place of great joy and freedom. On the monument to Dr Martin Luther King in Memphis, Tennessee, are these words from his last speech: "Free at last! Free at last! Thank God Almighty, I'm free at last!"

There was once a young widow who lived with

her son in a miserable attic. Several years before she had married against her parents' wishes and had gone with her husband to live in a foreign land. He had proved irresponsible and unfaithful, and after a few years he died without having made any provision for his wife and child. However, with the utmost difficulty she managed the scrape together the bare necessities of life.

The boy was happiest when his mother took him in her arms and told him about her father's house in the old country. She told him of the grassy lawn, the beautiful trees, the wild flowers, the lovely pictures on the walls and the delicious meals. The child had never seen his grandfather's home, but to him it was the most wonderful place in all the world. He longed to be able to go and live there.

One day the postman knocked at the attic's door. He handed the mother a letter. She instantly recognised the handwriting on the envelope as her father's and with trembling fingers opened it. Inside was a cheque and a slip of paper bearing just two words: "Come home."

For those who know God through Jesus, death is like that – it is going Home. What joy and happiness there is in the thought that one day we will leave this world and will go to be with Jesus!

An added joy is that in heaven we will meet again our loved ones who have already passed away:

> We'll meet again – perhaps today –
> The dear ones who have passed away;
> Oh, wondrous joy to meet them there
> At that blest union in the air!

Of course, there is a good deal of humour attached to the subject of death. There are many jokes about it. An Irish coroner once reported that "There are many people dying this year who never died before." A watchmaker's gravestone bore the inscription, "Stopped"; a sailor's said, "Reached harbour"; a fireman's said, "Burned out"; a mountaineer's said, "He died climbing"; a pessimist's said, "I told you so!" On the stone of a nagging wife were the words, "Here lies Enid Sour, whose conversation never ceased, but who now rests in peace." Woody Allen was once asked if he were afraid to die. He replied, "No, I'm not, but I don't want to be there when it happens!" Someone once said that there are six stages to a man's life: spills, drills, thrills, bills, ills and wills.

As he went to the scaffold in 1683 that great Englishman, Sir William Russell, took his watch from his pocket and handed it to the doctor who was attending him in his death. "Kindly take my timepiece," he said. "I have no use for it – I am now dealing with eternity." Like him, we shall all face eternity one day. If we are Christians, we will spend it in the presence of God; if not, we will spend it out of His presence. Everyone needs to be sure that he has prepared himself for death. Only receiving Christ as Saviour and Lord is adequate preparation.

A court jester was called to the presence of his king to cheer him up. But nothing the jester said or did had the least effect on the monarch's mood. Puzzled, the jester asked, "Why are you so sad, my Lord?"

"Because I have to leave my home and my people to go on a very long journey," replied the king.

"When will the journey begin, Sire?"

"I do not know, but quite soon, I think."

"But I see no clothes laid out, no boxes, no horses in the courtyard."

"I have been too busy to make preparations."

"Take my cap and bells," said the jester. "I thought I was the court fool, but I see there is here a greater fool than I! He is about to go on a long journey and yet calls me here to beguile his precious moments, when he could instead be preparing for his travels."

There are many people in real life who are like that king. They know that one day, perhaps soon, they will go on the long journey which is death, and yet instead of preparing themselves for it they waste their time on idle diversions.

Job declared, "Man's days are determined; you [God] have decreed the number of his months and have set limits he cannot exceed" (Job 14:5). Life is short, and we never know when death may come. In November 1975 the huge freighter *Edmund Fitzgerald* sank in the cold waters of Lake Superior during a fierce storm. Twenty-nine crewmen perished. One of those who died was Chief Steward Robert Rafferty. Only a week before the tragedy he had sent a postcard to his wife, saying, "I may be home on November 8. However, nothing is ever sure." Human life is so fragile. James said, "Why, you do not even know what will happen tomorrow. What is your life? You are a mist that appears for a little while and then vanishes" (James 4:14).

One day we will all meet Jesus face to face. If we have accepted Him as Saviour and Lord, He will say to us, "Come, you who are blessed by my Father;

take your inheritance, the kingdom prepared for you" (Matthew 25:34). If we have never received Him, He will say to us, "Depart from me, you who are cursed, into the eternal fire" (verse 41). Trust Christ for your salvation, and know the joyous certainty of an eternal life in the presence of God. As Paul says, "The gift of God is eternal life in Christ Jesus our Lord" (Romans 6:23). It's never too early to accept Christ, but at any moment it could be too late.

> Life is uncertain,
> Death is sure,
> Sin is the cause,
> Christ the cure!

PART II
THE CHRISTIAN LIFE

11. God Cares About You

I cast my eyes over the contents of the small room in the bare little cottage in the heart of Dorest. There was a firm leather lounger bed, clearly Arab in style. On the walls were photographs of desert scenes. Above the open coal fire were some cooking utensils of the sort that would normally be used by someone living a camping, outdoors lifestyle. On the bookshelf was a Bible, a Koran and a few other volumes. I made my way up the narrow, creaky, wooden stairs to the only bedroom. Here too the furnishings were simple and sparse. In the corner, hanging on a hook, was the "uniform" that told the whole story of the late occupant of the cottage: an Arab gown with a shawl and hood. It was white, but faded with age. It had belonged to one of my heroes – the strange, enigmatic character named T. E. Lawrence, popularly known as Lawrence of Arabia.

Lawrence had an adventurous and amazing life. He played a central part in the defeat of the vast forces of the Turkish war machine in the Middle East during the First World War. A young lieutenant in the British Army in Egypt, he volunteered to do liaison work and to seek to contact the wild, nomadic tribes of Arabia in order to gather information for Army intelligence. He finally managed to get a group of Arabs to agree to take him to meet their leader. To get to him they had to cross an extremely hot and inhospitable stretch of desert.

At one point in this journey the party realised that one of their number had got left behind at some stage. The straggler was a young Arab boy from one of the "lower", poorer tribes, so to the other Arabs he was a worthless individual. They would not have bothered to go back for him if he had been only yards behind, but he was in fact twenty-five miles behind! Then a sand storm blew up. No Arab travels in such a storm – he simply huddles down and waits for it to pass. But Lawrence was determined to return for the lost boy. In the Arabs' thinking this would have been an idiotic thing to do at any time, but to do it during a storm was sheer suicidal madness! Off Lawrence went, and the Arabs laughed. How could he risk his life for a mere insignificant boy? They were convinced that they would never see him again. After many hours the storm ended and the Arabs pressed on, having almost forgotten Lawrence. They had been travelling for about a day when they heard a cry behind them. There were two figures in the distance – it was Lawrance and the boy!

To Lawrence the life of a mere servant boy was of such value that he even risked his own life to save him. The Arabs were deeply impressed by this, and from that time onwards accepted him as one of themselves and looked upon him as almost a prophet. He raised a huge army from among these fierce desert tribesmen and captured the supposedly impregnable Turkish fortress of Aquaba without any British help — in fact without the generals even knowing about it! Then he and his army swept through the Middle East and took Damascus before General Allenby could even get there. Lawrence was a truly remarkable man. What made him great was his personal touch. With it he won the respect and allegiance of the tough desert people.

In these days of the mass society, we often feel that we are just numbers rather than people. Personal identity seems to be under threat. Each day at my office in Chippenham my staff answer numerous telephone calls from sick people or from the friends or relatives of those who are ailing. They ask us for help, and often they also ask if I will be able to see them *personally*. Will I myself be able to lay hands on them and pray for them? People of this generation are not used to having someone take a personal interest in them.

Thank God that Jesus came from heaven personally for us. "For God so loved the world that he gave his one and only Son, that whoever believes in him shall not perish but have eternal life" (John 3:16). A woman at a well, a blind man named Bartimaeus, a dishonest tax collector named Zacchaeus, a woman caught in adultery, a paralysed man at Bethesda, a prodigal son making his stumbling, heart-burdened way home — all of these individuals were important to Jesus.

We can be sure that in this selfish, uncaring, troubled, rat-race world, there is one place where *you are important, where you are personally cared for and loved, where you are not a mere number but a real person.* And that place is in the heart and mind of Jesus. That place in the Saviour's heart can be as real for you today as it was for those for whom He cared personally when He walked upon earth in the flesh.

12. God's Perfect Plan for Your Life

The building of the Panama Canal was a formidable task because of the difficult terrain through which it had to pass. Matters were made worse by the mosquitoes which infested the area. This great project could not have been accomplished without the remarkable courage and determination of the men who worked on it. They tackled the job with great spirit. For example, each workman had a plan of the completed canal next to his bunk so that he had a visible goal towards which to strive. The men were also inspired by what became known as *The Panama Song*:

> If you have rivers they say are uncrossable
> Or mountains you cannot tunnel through,
> We are specialists in the wholly impossible,
> Doing the thing that nobody can do.

They had a great plan, and they worked against every hindrance and obstacle until it was realised.

George Tomlinson, a young cotton weaver, believed that God was calling him to train for the ministry. He started getting up at 1.30 every morning to study before putting in ten hours of hard work at the mill. He was very disappointed when he was not accepted for the ministry, but he did not become bitter. Instead he looked for other ways in which to serve his fellow man. He entered politics and eventually became the Secretary of State for Education. He applied his Christian values to his work in this office and thus wielded a great influence for good. He had discovered God's plan for his life, and it was not quite what he had expected it to be.

I vividly remember the day when I arrived in the tiny Lincolnshire town of Horncastle. I had come to fill in for a minister who had been unable to make it to a healing crusade which he was to have led. This was the first crusade I had ever been involved in, and I was literally trembling with fear as I walked down the main street of the town. But during the two weeks of the campaign over a hundred people were saved. I was merely a substitute for someone else; I had no idea that the crusade would be so blessed by God! Ever since that time I have been caught up in a worldwide Gospel mission. God had a plan for me, even though I could not see it clearly at the beginning.

Have you found God's plan for your life? He has promised to guide us so that we fulfil His purposes for us. He has said, "I will instruct you and teach you in the way you should go; I will counsel you and watch over you" (Psalm 32:8). "I know the plans I have for you . . . plans to prosper you and not to harm you, plans to give you hope and a future" (Jeremiah 29:11).

A traveller once asked someone for directions. "How far away am I from my destination?" he asked.

"Thousands of miles!" was the reply.

"But I know it's just a few miles away," said the puzzled traveller.

"Yes, that's right, but you're going in the wrong direction. If you carry on that way you'll have to go all around the world to get to your destination!"

Perhaps your back is turned towards God's plan for your life. If so, it will take you a very long time to find it!

Two men were looking at a painting of a harbour scene in the National Gallery. Pointing to the fishermen who were idly sitting or strolling about, one of the men remarked, "This picture should be called *The Micawbers*! Look at them – they're all just waiting for something to turn up!" "But don't you see the mended nets and the boats which are all ready to set sail?" said the other man. "The fishermen have got everything ready, and they are now waiting for the tide to turn." We sometimes need to do what those fishermen did. There are times when there is nothing more for us to do: we have prepared ourselves and have done everything we can, and all we can now do is to wait for the turn of the tide. We must wait for God to speak and to show His plan to us. He will always reveal Himself in the end to the seeking heart.

God often reveals His plan to us in the dark and difficult times in our lives. At a time of great need in his life Isaiah saw the Lord "seated on a throne, high and exalted" (Isaiah 6:1). A live coal touched his lips and he received his calling. Thus he found out God's purpose for his life.

During a visit to Belgium the late Dr Don Gray Barnhouse went into a shop to buy some lace for his wife. He asked to see a sample, expecting that the lace would simply be placed on the counter so that he could look at it. But no, when one is buying expensive lace it is placed on a large black cushion. Only when it is on such a background can its intricate beauty be clearly seen. In a similar way, God's wonderful plans for us are often placed against a dark backdrop so that we may perceive them.

Colin Urquhart calls some believers "billiard-ball Christians", because they get knocked about, rolling from here to there with no coordination, plan or purpose. God doesn't want His people to be like that. He has redeemed us; we are worth a great deal to Him, and He has plans for us. We can have full confidence in Him. His Word says, "So do not throw away your confidence; it will be richly rewarded" (Hebrews 10:35).

I love to see confidence in Christians, because it can enable them to achieve great things for God. If ever I am tempted to doubt that someone can ever do anything much for the Lord, I think about a story I once heard about Sir Arthur Conan Doyle, the creator of Sherlock Holmes. He was once chatting with a young actor who was at that time earning just a few shillings a week playing a part in one of Sir Arthur's plays. The actor was a nobody, but with tongue in cheek he suggested that the famous Sir Arthur and he should pool their incomes and share the total equally for the rest of their days. Of course, Sir Arthur didn't take him seriously. After all, he had no time to waste on a cocksure, cheeky little whipper-snapper . . . *whose name happened to be Charlie Chaplin!* Confidence in Christ is something like that. We may seem insignificant, but if we trust Him He can use us mightily. Of course, our confidence in Jesus should not make us cocky, boastful, brash or disrespectful. Instead we should be *humbly* confident. We must yield to whatever God reveals to us, even if we don't like all that He says to us.

A while ago I read in a magazine that when two mountain goats meet in a very narrow defile or on a rocky ledge, where there is no room to pass and where to go back might be difficult or even fatal, one of the goats lies down while the other walks over it. Sadly, human beings often fail to display this sort of good sense. They refuse to swallow their pride and give way. As a result they cause a great deal of trouble for themselves.

We need to submit to God; we need to lie down and let Him walk over us. If we do that He will reward us and bless us. His plan for our lives will unfold and He will show us the way to peace, power, fruitfulness, joy, success and prosperity. He will show us the way forward: "He will guard the feet of his saints" (1 Samuel 2:9).

All that God requires of us is submission and obedience. His Word says, "be careful to do what the Lord your God has commanded you; do not turn aside to the right or to the left. Walk in all the way that the Lord your God has commanded you, so that you may live long and prosper" (Deuteronomy 5:32-33). God's plan is yours for the asking. He will not fail you.

13. God Keeps His Promises

I had just returned home after being away for some weeks on a mission. My son Philip came to me and reminded me that I had promised to take him to see a Donald Duck film at the cinema that evening. I told him I was too tired to go out. "But you promised me, Dad!" he protested, tears on his cheeks. As I looked at his sad face my conscience rebuked me. So I gave in and took him to see the film after all. Children expect their parents to keep their promises, and rightly so.

Some people's promises aren't worth much, because we know that they probably won't keep them. However, God always keeps His promises. In the Bible there are 7,487 promises made by God personally! The missionary Adoniram Judson used to say, "The future is as bright as the promises of God." He eagerly claimed God's promises, and as a result there is a rapidly growing church in Burma today. Man may be unreliable, but God is absolutely reliable. Scripture says, "the Lord our God . . . remembers his covenant for ever, the word he commanded, for a thousand generations" (Psalm 105:7-8). It also says, "For the Lord your God is a merciful God; he will not abandon or destroy you or forget the covenant with your forefathers, which he confirmed to them by oath" (Deuteronomy 4:31).

God has promised "to meet all your needs according to his glorious riches in Christ Jesus" (Philippians 4:19). Another translation of this verse reads, "Out of the greatness of his wealth he will give to us." What a wonderful promise! I can testify that He has never failed to meet all my needs. On four occasions in my life God has kept this promise in a truly miraculous way. Three of those miracles occurred some time ago when I was working in Malaysia. The fourth happened about four years ago when I was doing church-planting work in a rural area of France. There were no evangelical churches in the district and the local people had shown little interest in the Gospel message. However, there had been an encouraging trickle of converts. There came a time when I badly needed some money to live on. I carefully counted what I had left – just fifty francs. I put the money in my case and locked it for safety. No-one could possibly open the case without knowing the code. Later, wondering how I was going to manage with so little money, I opened the case again and was amazed and delighted to discover that there were now two hundred and fifty francs in it! It was an outright miracle.

How can one fail to trust a God who does things like that? Of course, He doesn't always keep His promises in such an obviously miraculous way, but He does always keep them. However, in return He requires us to obey Him. Queen Elizabeth I asked a great admiral, who had served her loyally and bravely and had now retired to an estate in the country, to undertake one more special and dangerous voyage for her. He tried to excuse himself from this, saying, "I have my land, workers and business to attend to." The Queen replied, "You see to my business, and I will take care of yours!" Jesus our Lord has promised that if we do our part and obey Him, He will do His part and take care of us.

During a very exciting healing crusade in West Wales a little girl was brought to me. She had a sweet face but she was scruffily dressed and was in need of a good wash. I was very busy and asked an assistant to deal with the matter. He replied that it was serious, since someone had seen the girl take a pound coin out of the collection. I was shown the coin, and I asked her if she had stolen it.

"No!" she replied.

A teenager standing beside her stated that she had seen her deliberately put her hand in the collection basket and take the coin out. My assistant supported this allegation and added that he had found the coin in her hand. I questioned the girl again:

"You say you didn't steal it. But it was in your hand — so where did you get it from?"

"Out of the collection basket!" she replied perkily.

I was confused. "So you did steal it, then?"

"Oh no, I didn't!" she retorted. "When you were here in this church a couple of years ago you told the people to give generously. And you said that if we were poor and didn't have anything to give and needed money ourselves, then we should take a pound out of the basket. So that's what I did tonight!"

I laughed with relief, and marvelled that a child

should have remembered that offer I had made a few years ago.

"So what should we do?" asked my assistant.

"Let her go," I said. "She's done nothing wrong. She just took me at my word!"

We Christians should treat God that way — we should take Him at His Word, because He is a loving Father who always keeps His promises!

14. Prayer – The Way to Power

Through persistent prayer the power of God is released in our lives, in the lives of others and in the life of our nation. The celebrated preacher Smith Wigglesworth often prayed well into the small hours of the morning. The Puritans held four prayer meetings every day of the year, and for a time they took control of England! The daughter of a minister once told a friend, "When my father's trousers got threadbare at the knees, it was always a sure sign that revival was on its way." Former Archbishop of Canterbury Donald Coggan once said, "When a man or woman is praying the appropriate notice is not so much 'Quiet! Man at prayer!' as 'Look out! God at work!'"

Prayer never fails to astonish me! It is health-producing and power-generating; it restores and recreates us, it increases and exercises our love for others. It makes us Godlike – it makes our hearts throb with His love and power.

When we pray we are meeting with the Living God. There would be no point in praying to Shakespeare or Napoleon – they are just dead men, and they cannot hear us or help us. But Jesus Christ is the One who died and rose again, and He is alive today and forever! We cry to Him, "Dear Jesus, melt me, change me, cleanse me! I praise and glorify You! Hear my cry — answer me, Lord!" He hears us and He never fails to answer our prayers.

As I have driven home late at night from meetings and campaigns in different parts of the country I have often seen young people streaming home from discos and nightclubs, sometimes as late as three in the morning. The sinners have been worshipping their false gods, who will in the end destroy them. *Where are the believers who pray into the small hours, beseeching God to revive the land?* I often pray, "O God, get this unbelieving generation of Christians on their knees!"

People are dying without the bread of life. We must look to the spiritual welfare of the unsaved people around us, we must throw God's light on the dark places in our land. We must offer people new hope instead of their utter *hopelessness*. What has the world to offer them? Nothing. We must point the hungry masses to God and to the heavenly city of which He is the builder and maker. We must call the people out of their lostness, coldness, barrenness, darkness and bleakness into the light, warmth and laughter of the Kingdom of God.

The spiritual climate goes through different seasons, but we must be constant. We must never give up. We must pray, pray, pray. We must seek revival and build, build, build. We must live in the fear of the Almighty and put His will and His Great Commission first in our lives.

But when we pray we first need to make sure that our hearts are right with God. The Psalmist said, "the Lord God is a sun and shield; the Lord bestows favour and honour; no good thing does he withhold from those whose walk is blameless" (Psalm 84:11). We must be right with God if we are to receive what we ask for in prayer.

In one of his last sermons the famous Amercian evangelist D. L. Moody preached from this Psalm. After the service a woman asked him to pray that her husband might be converted. She said she had been concerned about him for many years.

"I will pray with you for him on one condition," Moody told her, "and that is that you have fulfilled the requirement of verse 11 of Psalm 84. Tell me, are you walking uprightly?"

After some thought she confessed, "I'm afraid I'm not."

Moody told her, "Ask God to forgive the past and save you from your besetting sins, and then promise that you will do His will."

The woman got down on her knees immediately and admitted her own shortcomings and got right with God. Moody then prayed earnestly for her husband's salvation. The very next day the man turned to God. Moody had previously seen many similar, almost miraculous answers to prayer result when those seeking God's blessing had fully met the conditions of Psalm 84.

When we pray we do not come to God as beggars and vagabonds but as His children, as the heirs to His infinite wealth and boundless resources. Scripture promises us that in response to our sincere, earnest, heart-of-heart prayers God will supply all of our needs "according to his glorious riches in

Christ Jesus" (Philippians 4:19). God supplies our needs richly because He has endless riches from which to supply them. He answers our prayers plenteously, gloriously and liberally!

A man once visited a stately home that was open to the public. He was greatly impressed by the beautiful and fascinating paintings, furniture, valuables and suits of armour. However, in one room he noticed that on a chess table there were two items that were not listed in the official catalogue. He asked the curator about this. The curator looked at the table and realised that the visitor was right. There was one ornament of solid gold and one of solid silver. Both were very valuable. He was baffled.

"Well, that's strange," he said, scratching his head. "They weren't there last night!"

"How do you think they got there?" asked the visitor.

"I think the master of the house must have come in last night and left them here for us," decided the curator.

Out of his great riches the wealthy master had put out a few extra items for the pleasure, education and inspiration of the visitors.

Our Heavenly Master is like that. He has an infinite storehouse of riches, and so He always has something more to share with us and give to us. He always answers prayer and we can never ask too much of Him. God said to Abram, "I am your shield, your very great reward" (Genesis 15:1). He is our very great reward too. We have only to ask, and He will reward our asking. *Ask, ask, ask and keep on asking!*

15. Listening to God

A young man's Ford Model T had broken down. He pushed it off the road and spent hours trying to fix it, without success. Then a large Ford car drew to a stop behind his car and a tall, well-dressed man got out.

"Can I help at all?" he asked.

The young man was in a very bad mood by now and simply ignored the man. He continued to work on the car for a while, but finally threw the spanner down in frustration and gave up. Looking up, he noticed that the other man was still there beside the car.

"Okay, you have a go, then!" said the young man rudely. "But I bet you can't do it! I bet you don't know the first thing about cars. You've probably never once got your hands dirty in your whole life!"

The other man said nothing and opened the bonnet. He adjusted one or two things inside, then got in the car and started it on the first attempt. The young man was amazed, and went and thanked him.

"How did you do that?" he asked. "You got my car started in no time at all!"

"I'm Henry Ford," said the man, smiling.

He was the maker of the car, so he knew

everything there was to know about it. Fixing it was a simple matter for him.

There is a message for us Christians in this story. God is our Maker, so He, more than anyone else, knows how we are made, how we work and what we need to keep us in good working order. In order to live rightly and successfully we need God's guidance. We need to listen to our Maker and do as He says.

However, listening to God often proves to be a problem for us. The famed Joan of Arc claimed that God visited her and that she heard Him speak to her with an audible voice. When she met the King of France for the first time, he said to her, "I am the King of France, but I have never heard the voice of God!" Joan replied quietly, "But if you will listen, O King, then you will hear Him speak."

The American songwriter Frank Loesser wrote a number of well-known musicals, including the immensely popular *Guys and Dolls*, *Where's Charlie?* and *The Most Happy Fella*. Once, in an interview, he was asked where he got the ideas for his songs from. "Oh, they just pop into my head!" he replied. Then he added, "Of course, my head happens to be correctly arranged to receive songs. Some people's heads are arranged so that they keep getting colds, but I keep getting songs!" Well, I don't suppose it was really quite as easy as that, but it is true that a head that is "arranged" – or perhaps we should say a heart that is "attuned" – to receive certain things does seem to attract those things to itself. Gloomy thoughts attract more thoughts of the same kind, but a heart attuned to beauty, goodness, kindness and happiness acts as a kind of magnet, so that those sorts of thoughts keep "popping into" a person's head. Similarly, if our hearts are attuned to God's voice, we will hear Him.

For over thirty years Dora Oliver was the water bailiff on a stretch of the River Dove in Derbyshire, just like her father before her. She was also at one time a celebrated concert pianist. She gave this up in later life, but she still had her music. She was once interviewed for television. She and the interviewer were walking along the riverbank when she stopped and said, "Listen to that weir! How it sings!"

"Sings?" said the interviewer.

"Yes," she replied. "Everything makes music – the river, the breeze, the reeds. There's music everywhere. But people need to have ears which can hear it."

We need to have ears which can hear God's voice!

Sometimes we are prevented from hearing His voice because it is being drowned out by something else. A little boy was reading his Bible at home one day. His father had the radio on at a rather high volume. "Please turn the radio down, Dad," asked the boy. "I can't hear God speaking to me!"

I'm not quite old enough to remember the days when sermons were timed by an hourglass in the pulpit, but I do recall thinking as a small boy that what we called the "long prayer" in the church services seemed to go on for hours! However, prayers need not be very long. The late Dr W. E. Sangster, the well-known Methodist preacher, used to speak of what he called "minute prayers" – brief prayers "shot out" from the heart to God at any moment of the day. By such prayers we can keep in constant touch with Him and retain a sense of His presence. Sangster used to say that a great deal of prayer could be contained in just a few words. We may well find that some of our most meaningful prayers are of this kind — it may be a verse from a hymn, a sentence of Scripture, a simple request or confession or thanksgiving. If our prayers are too long, we don't allow ourselves any time to listen to God. Someone once said, "God gave us two ears but only one mouth; therefore we ought to listen much and speak little." O God, help us to listen to You more!

An inquiring little boy once asked his mother what it was to be wise, and so she sent him to a wise man who lived nearby. The boy asked him what the secret of his wisdom was. "Listen," said the old man. The boy waited with bated breath for more, but there was no more to come. The heart of the old man's wisdom lay in that one little word.

It is indeed wise to listen. The greatest wisdom of all is to listen to God.

16. When God is Silent

One Sunday morning a lady was sitting in her garden
in a mood of deep depression. A number of things
in her life had been going badly recently. God seemed
a long way off and silent. Then the bells in the tower
of the local church started to ring, summoning the
people to worship. They were playing the tune of
the hymn which begins, "Holy, holy, holy, Lord God
Almighty, early in the morning our songs shall rise
to Thee." As the woman listened her mood changed.
It seemed as though the music of the bells had lifted
a curtain, allowing her to see all the good things that
she had in her life. Indeed, their message so touched
her that when she met the minister of the church a
few days later she handed him a gift to be given to
the bellringer. She had thought that God was silent,
but He had spoken to her heart through the bells.

In chapter 6 of Mark's Gospel (verses 45 – 52) we
read that Jesus told the disciples to cross over the
Sea of Galilee in a boat so that they would get to
Bethsaida ahead of him. Once they had set off He
went into the hills to pray. The wind was against
the disciples. They struggled with the oars for over
nine hours and in that time covered only three miles!
Their situation must have seemed hopeless to them.

Eventually Jesus walked out to them on the water, calming both the wind and their fears. However, throughout the nine hours, from His vantage point in the hills, He had been able to see the disciples' predicament. Why did He not come and help them sooner? Why the delay?

I believe the reason was this: Jesus wanted to convince the disciples that He had power from God. He had just miraculously fed five thousand people with just a few loaves and fish, but, as Mark (chapter 6) comments, "they had not understood about the loaves; their hearts were hardened" (verse 52). They had not perceived the miracle, and so they needed a forceful demonstration of His power. They could not fail to notice His ability to walk on water and calm the wind! Sometimes we need a good shaking to make us realise what a great God we have!

In the next chapter of Mark's Gospel (verses 24–30) we read that Jesus "entered a house and did not want anyone to know it". He did not go to the woman with the demon-possessed child – rather, she came to Him and fell at His feet. Why was He secretive? However, He granted her request, and when she returned home she found that her child was free from the demon.

What are we to make of the fact that when Jesus heard that His friend Lazarus was ill, He didn't immediately go to Bethany? John says, "when he heard that Lazarus was sick, he stayed where he was two more days" (John 11:6). He didn't delay because He was preoccupied with prayer at the time. It seems that the delay was deliberate.

When Jesus finally arrived at Bethany, Martha and Mary complained that if He had been there at the time of their brother's sickness he would not have died. Jesus went to the tomb and ordered its entrance stone to be removed. "But, Lord," protested Martha, "by this time there is a bad odour, for he has been there four days." But Jesus' order was obeyed, and then He commanded Lazarus to come out of the tomb.

What did He prove by this? Perhaps He wanted to demonstrate that the power of God in Him could overcome not only death but physical decomposition too!

God was silent when Joseph, the young man with so many marvellous visions and dreams, was sold by his brothers; He was silent too when he was thrown into an Egyptian prison cell. But God eventually brought Joseph out of prison and made him Pharaoh's right-hand man!

Job lost his home, his family, his wealth, his health, his public esteem – everything. God explained none of this to him; He was silent. But in the end He healed Job and made him twice as prosperous as he had ever been before.

We should notice that in all five of the biblical examples we have looked at, blessing eventually followed God's delay and seeming silence. The people had to wait for God to act, but in the end they had the answers to their prayers. The lesson we have to learn from all this is that *God's delays are not His denials*.

Do you sometimes feel frustrated by God's delays and silences? Do you sometimes feel that He is ignoring you? You are not alone! Most believers experience this at some time or other. It is one of most difficult aspects of Christian living. When the notable evangelist David Watson lay dying of cancer, just fifty-one years of age, the Bishop of Southwark wrote: "One of the great mysteries we have to live with is the silences of God."

When I experience those trying times when I taste the bitter cup and see no apparent answers to my prayers, I adopt this attitude: I take it that He is in favour of what I have prayed, that He is saying "Yes" to it. Only when I hear a definite "No" from God do I stop and change course. During thirty-six years of preaching and walking with God, I have found that this is the only way to beat the frustration I feel as a result of God's delays.

Derek Bingham has wisely said that God's delayed answers to prayer are "the quickest way to blessing. In every delay there is a purpose and an answer bigger and better than anything you could ever have asked for. This fact is true, and the quicker we learn it the less we will be frustrated."

17. Light in the Darkness

As he was driving through Kent to North London a friend of mine was listening to a thrilling "whodunnit" play on the radio. He was enthralled by the suspense and wondered who the culprit was. He had been really gripped by the story by the time he reached the Dartford Tunnel. Suddenly his radio went silent as it was cut off from the broadcast by the roof of the tunnel. He had a "Sunday driver" in front of him, moving at about twenty miles per hour. Overtaking is not allowed in the tunnel, so he had to crawl along, biting his nails, wondering what the outcome of the play would be. Finally he reached the end of the tunnel and the radio picked up the signal again. My friend was dismayed to find that by now the closing music was being played and the credits were being read out. He had missed the end of the play! To this day he doesn't know "whodunnit"!

In a similar way, many people in our world are lost in a tunnel of darkness, cut off from communication with God. They don't know why they are here or where they are going to. Many are in a dark night of despair, sickness, worry, debt, financial strains, family cares, personality problems, oppressions and depressions.

The story is told of the electricity meter reader who called at a tiny cottage at the end of a rough track in a Scottish glen. Having read the meter carefully he exclaimed, "You've only used three units! Do you never use electricity?" "I do that," said the old man who lived alone in the cottage. "I put it on every night while I find the matches and light the lamps, and I put it on for a moment at bedtime when I put the lamps out!" What a pity to have all that light at one's fingertips and to live in semidarkness! Many people are only a prayer away from a miracle, from an answer to their problems, from full light and release in their lives, from joy and forgiveness, and yet they live in the shadows.

If we seek Him, we will find God amidst the darkness of our lives. At the outbreak of the Second World War the King of England read out in a radio broadcast some lines written by the Somerset poetess Minnie Haskins. They inspired millions of British people in those dark times:

> As you go into the darkness,
> Put your hand into the hand of God.
> This is better than any human light,
> And surer than any known way.

The Apostle John wrote, "God is light; in him there is no darkness at all" (1 John 1:5). Jesus called Himself "the light of the world" (John 8:12). When you receive Jesus into your life, His light comes in too. Paul wrote, "For God, who said, 'Let light shine out of darkness,' made his light shine in our hearts to give us the light of the knowledge of the glory of God in the face of Christ" (2 Corinthians 4:6).

God is light. One of our Royal family chose that inspired hymn, "Immortal, Invisible" for her wedding service. It is sometimes called "the hymn that makes the sun shine". It includes the words:

All laud we would render; O help us to see
'Tis only the splendour of light hideth Thee.

We Christians have God's light with us and within us. We are to take it out into the world. God wants us to be a saved, pure, holy, sanctified, Spirit-filled people, a light which will illuminate the whole earth for His glory.

18. Faltering Faith

Sometimes Christians find their faith faltering. Then they turn away from faith and start to rely on human endeavour and ability. If you take your eyes off God and abandon faith, you soon become a tragic shadow of what you were. For you spiritual exploits and victories and miracles become things of the past. That is what has happened to the modern Church.

King David tasted this bitter experience in his lifetime. When his life was threatened by King Saul his faith slipped. "There is only a step between me and death," he told his friend Jonathan, Saul's son (1 Samuel 20:3). That was the way it seemed to him at the time, but in fact it was very far from the truth. Indeed, God had promised him that he was to be the King of Israel. And yet now he took his eyes off that promise, and his faith faltered as a result.

His life still under threat from Saul, David went to a quiet highland village called Nob. There was a sanctuary there where eighty-six priests lived. When he arrived a priest named Ahimelech asked him, "Why are you alone?" (1 Samuel 21:2). It is sad to have to write that David, in a state of panic, lied. He said he was on secret business for King Saul and was meeting up with his men later. Oh, what tangled webs we weave when first we practice to deceive!

David asked Ahimelech if he had a sword anywhere. Did he have a sword? That's like asking your local preacher if he has any guns in his house! The priest replied, "The sword of Goliath the Philistine, whom you killed in the valley of Elah, is here; it is wrapped in a cloth behind the ephod. If you want it, take it; there is no sword here but that one" (verse 9). When people panic their faith is often eclipsed. David had not needed a sword to defeat the giant Goliath, but he felt he needed one to defend himself against King Saul. So the sword which had been in the sanctuary for years as a trophy of his faith now went in his hand as a symbol of the collapse of that faith. He said to the priest, "There is none like it; give it to me." Those have got to be some of the saddest words in the Old Testament.

Down, down, down went David – down to Gath, down to live among the Philistines, down to act the madman. There, in the presence of King Achish of Gath he feigned madness in order to protect himself, "making marks on the doors of the gate and letting saliva run down his beard". Achish exclaimed, "Look at the man! He is insane! Why bring him to me? Am I so short of madmen that you have to bring this fellow here to carry on like this in front of me?" (verses 13-15). David then escaped to the cave of Adullam. What a sad story!

David was in a sorry state. He was the man who had been especially chosen by God to be the King of Israel; he had been a man after God's own heart

– pure, sincere, kindly, good-hearted, full of faith
– and yet now he had deserted faith.

May we all learn the lessons which this sorry episode in David's life teaches us. Let us keep our eyes on God and on His promises. Let us not doubt Him when things become difficult in our lives. We should not, like David, look at God through the mists of circumstances, and so lose sight of Him. Instead we should look at circumstances through the promises of God.

19. Put the King in the Middle

A Chistian farmer was marking his sheep with his mark of ownership. A fellow Christian visiting the farm watched him doing this. Over a cup of tea afterwards the farmer said, "Christ's sheep are marked too, you know – on the ear and on the foot."

"Why do you say that?" asked his friend.

"Because Jesus said, 'My sheep listen to my voice; I know them, and they follow me.'" (See John 10:27.)

It is sadly the case that not all of Christ's sheep really listen to Him or really follow Him with true devotion. They cannot truly say that He is at the centre of their lives.

Luke records that when Jesus appeared to the disciples after His resurrection He "stood among them" (Luke 24:36), in the central place in the midst of them. When He was a boy His parents found Him in the Temple in Jerusalem, "sitting among the teachers, listening to them and asking them questions" (Luke 2:46). He had the central place even among the theologians. Wouldn't it be wonderful if that were the case today! Then there would be no more utterances like those of Bishop David Jenkins of Durham.

Put the King in the Middle

Two boys were having difficulty putting together a jigsaw puzzle which was meant to depict a royal procession. One looked hard at the picture on the box and said, "I see what we've been doing wrong! We must put the King in the middle." They did so, and then instead of a puzzle they had a picture. Likewise, we must put Christ, our King, in the middle of our lives – we must put Him first and let Him control us. He must be the influence which dominates our lifestyle.

Even those who are working hard for the Lord sometimes fail to put Him at the centre of things. It is possible for us to become so engrossed in our work for the Lord that we forget the Lord of the work! We need to have a clear vision of Christ before us at all times. We need to see Him crucified, raised from the dead and ascended to the right hand of God. If you have lost that vision, do whatever you have to do to recapture it. Do not succumb to the negative pessimism which infiltrates the Church today, but instead be restored to the sparkling purity and joy of the Gospel!

20. Be Prepared

We all know the old scouts' motto, "Be prepared".
It is just as relevant to adult life as to childhood. We
need to live in a state of preparedness. We need to
be ready for what God has in store for us, for
unexpected opportunities, challenges, demands,
stresses, problems and trials. Sometimes we have
"red letter days", and we must be ready if we are
not to waste the opportunites which they give us.
We must learn from God and from life; we must
wait, prepare, pray and develop ourselves, so that
we are ready for whatever God calls us to do in life.

The Bible often speaks about being prepared.
Proverbs advises us, "Finish your outdoor work and
get your fields ready; after that, build your house"
(24:27). Solomon said, "Blessed is the man who finds
wisdom, the man who gains understanding"
(Proverbs 3:13) – or in other words, "Happy is the
man who is well prepared"!

History teaches us to be prepared. When the
French government tried to call up their military
reserves in 1939 in the face of the threat from
Germany, they discovered to their horror that much
of those reserves exisited on paper only. They were
uprepared for the Germans when they invaded.

Be Prepared

A preacher visiting a country church was asked by the vicar if he would like any particular hymn to be sung in the service to complement his sermon. "No, no," he relied. "As a matter of fact, I hardly ever know what I'm going to say until I'm in the pulpit." "Oh, well, in that case," said the vicar, "perhaps we'd better have the hymn, 'For those at sea'."

On a more serious note, I know of an outstanding Scottish evangelist linked with the Elim churches who used to hold a "preparation" meeting before his evening service. There his congregation would be taught and encouraged and so prepared for the main meeting. This approach proved to be quite successful.

How often one hears people who are going through difficult times say, "If only I had been prepared for all this!" The famous French scientist Madame Curie achieved many great things for science. Her discovery of radium has been of enormous medical significance. However, she was an agnostic. One day her husband was killed in a street accident in Paris. When some friends carried his body into the Curies' home she became hysterical with grief. "How will I live now?" she screamed. "I have no faith!" None of her scientific knowledge and achievements could comfort her now. She was unprepared for death, the one inevitable thing in life. We Christians are prepared for death, but God asks us to prepare other people for it too. We must urge them to face up to the fact of death and to turn to Jesus, the only one who can save them from it.

Before beginning to sculpt the figure *David*,

Michelangelo first of all studied the character of the brave young shepherd boy. The artist asked himself, "When did David achieve greatness? Was it when he killed Goliath or when he decided to do it?" He concluded that it was the decision and not the slaying that made David a moral and spiritual giant. Look back on your own life. Haven't your greatest struggles taken place in your heart and mind? And isn't it there that your finest victories have been won? The secret of victory in life's battles is in our preparation for them.

You may have failed in something, and you feel despondent. But turn to God and His strength, and allow Him to prepare you for another try:

> When you have failed and failed and failed,
> Kneel where you are, and pray
> That God will give you strength and grace
> To win another day;
> With Him, in spite of grief or pain,
> You'll have the will to try again.

Sometimes we wonder where our lives are going. Your career or business may be going through a crucial phase which will decide its future course. You may not yet be able to clearly see the way ahead. Your life seems full of uncertainty. If that's the situation you're in at the moment, I want to assure you that I know just how you feel. I've often gone through times like that. The days drag by so very, very slowly, don't they? Sarah Doudney said,

> But the waiting time, my brothers,
> Is the hardest time of all.

There is no sure and easy way out of such a situation. All you can do is keep on waiting, praying and preparing. The Good Book says, "Whoever sows sparingly will also reap sparingly, and whoever sows generously will also reap generously" (2 Corinthians 9:6). We all need to sow for the times ahead, to invest in the future, to prepare ourselves and become better Christians.

Did you hear about the small girl who asked her father, "What does an 'L' on a car mean?" Her father explained that it meant that the driver was a learner. A day or two later she spotted a car with a "GB" sticker on its rear end. "Oh," she exclaimed, "that car must have a driver who is getting better!"

While learning to drive is a tricky business, learning to live successfully is even more difficult. It's a long process, too. We need to ensure that we're constantly getting better at it.

21. Be Merciful

During an interview on BBC radio a little while ago I was asked which virtue, in my opinion, had Western civilisation most thoroughly lost hold of. I surprised the interviewer by replying, "Mercy." It is one of the true tests of the quality of a society.

God's Word says, "The Lord your God is a merciful God" (Deuteronomy 4:31). Jesus has commanded us, "Be merciful, just as your Father is merciful" (Luke 6:36). He shows us mercy, and so we must show mercy to others — even our enemies. Jesus said, "If you love only those who love you, what credit is that to you?" (Matthew 5:46, J. B. Phillips). He also said, "Blessed are the merciful, for they will be shown mercy" (Matthew 5:7).

What does the word "merciful" mean? The thought behind it is that of compassion and concern for others. One authority, W. E. Vine, says that a "merciful" person is "not simply possessed of pity but is actively compassionate".

Prior to being the first citizen of New York City, Mayor La Guardia was a judge in a local court in a poor area of the city during the Great Depression of 1931. A man was brought before him for stealing a basketful of bread loaves. La Guardia asked him why he had done it. The man replied that he was unemployed and his family had been hungry. He had taken the bread in desperation. He was not a thief – he had never been in court before. The judge looked around the crowded courtroom. The people sat still and silent, waiting for his judgement. He told the man, "I fine you fifty dollars for this crime." There was a gasp from the onlookers. How could the impoverished man possibly pay such a sum? "But," continued the judge, "I fine everyone in this court half a dollar for allowing to exist the circumstances which forced this man to steal to feed his family." He ordered a court official to pass a couple of hats around. Once collected, the fifty dollars were handed to the man, who promptly paid his fine. There was clapping and cheering in the courthouse. The man went free and was never seen in court again!

La Guardia chose mercy rather than punishment. No wonder he later became New York's greatest and most beloved Mayor and the city's International Airport was named after him.

An American nurse and her brother were working in Turkey. One evening they went out for a walk. Suddenly they were attacked by a gang of Turks, who killed the nurse's brother before her eyes. The gang escaped and were never apprehended. Some months later, while on duty at the hospital where she worked, she recognised one of her patients as the man who had murdered her brother. Her first feeling was a desire for revenge. The man was extremely ill, hanging between life and death. She realised that with the slightest neglect on her part he would die. His life was absolutely in her hands. But she was a Christian, so she decided for Christ's sake to forgive the man rather than seek revenge. She fought for his life and won, nursing him back to health.

When he recovered she told him who she was. The man looked at her in astonishment and said, "Why didn't you let me die when you had me in your power?"

"I just couldn't," she replied. "I am a Christian, and my Master forgave His enemies who crucified Him. I must do the same for His sake."

"Well," said the Turk, "if this is what it means to be a Christian, then I want to be one too!"

Could you and I do what that nurse did? It isn't easy, but it can be done – with God's help. The ability to be merciful is not something which arises from our natural temperament. Rather, it is something with which we are endowed when we abide in Christ.

The mother of a little girl who was murdered by Hindley and Brady, the infamous child killers, was for over twenty years full of hatred and a desire for revenge. But then she became a Christian, and so was able to forgive the murderers. This shows that mercy and forgiveness come from God. The poet Pope expressed it thus: "To err is human, to forgive is divine."

One of Napoleon's soldiers – a nineteen year-old boy – was found sleeping on guard duty and was sentenced to death for it. The day before his execution his mother came to Napoleon's headquarters to plead for his life. Somehow she managed to get an audience with the great man himself. He listened silently to her plea.

"Madame," he said, "do you think your son deserves mercy?"

The little woman drew herself up and looked him in the eye fearlessly. "Sir," she replied quietly, "if he deserved it, it would not be mercy."

It is said that Napoleon was so impressed by her courage and dignity that he pardoned the boy. What is more, he went on to beome one of Napoleon's most brave and loyal men. Finally he died in batle, giving his own life to save Napoleon's.

God is merciful to us, as David declares In Psalm 23, the great Shepherd's Psalm: "Surely goodness and mercy shall follow me all the days of my life" (verse 6, AV). A mother read this psalm to her little boy one bedtime and told him all about the Good Shepherd.

"What were the names of his sheepdogs?" asked the boy.

"I don't think the Shepherd had any," replied his mother.

"But how could he have looked after all those sheep without any sheepdogs?"

The boy settled down to sleep, thinking about this. In the morning he announced to his mother, "I know the names of the sheepdogs! They were called Goodness and Mercy!"

22. "Look at All the Lonely People . . ."

"I am so lonely. I just don't know what to do with myself. Since my wife died the loneliness has been dreadful. I try to fill up my days, but – oh! – the emptiness . . ."

I have heard sad words like those more times than I can remember. The great C. S. Lewis wrote, "As soon as we are fully conscious we discover loneliness." It is a disease as old as the hills. Christopher Columbus said, "I found no island or quay so lonely as myself." One of the Beatles' famous songs goes:

> Look at all the lonely people –
> Where do they all come from? . . .
> Where do they all belong?

Shortly after Queen Victoria's husband Albert died in 1861, she described her feelings of loneliness to a friend: "Always wishing to consult one who is not here, groping with myself, with a constant sense of desolation." Albert had been her companion for twenty-one years, and now that he was no longer with her she felt a crushing sense of emptiness.

Experiences such as bereavement, illness or catastrophe can make us feel acutely lonely. Heavy clouds of despair roll over us. At times like that we need help.

People can be lonely in the most unexpected of places. I myself was never so lonely as when I was the odd man out at a party. I was only eighteen. Everybody there knew everybody else, but no-one knew me. In the end I slipped quietly away. That was a silly thing to do, I admit, but I felt less lonely going home in the dark than I had felt at the lively party.

Nearly 125 years ago a young American singer and composer named Hart Danks sat in his room looking over some verses that had been sent to him. As he read them he felt his heart quicken, for they spoke to him of all that he felt about his own wife, about the comfort he and she would be to each other when they grew old. Right away he took up his pen and began to write the song which was already forming in his mind. It went like this:

> Darling, I am growing old.
> Silver threads among the gold
> Shine upon my brow today,
> Life is fading fast away . . .

It was a beautiful song and became very popular. I would like to be able to tell you that all the happiness it promised came true for Danks and his wife. Alas, it was not to be. They parted, and for the last thirty years of his life he was a lonely, broken man. He died in a Philedelphia boarding house in 1903. His landlady found a copy of the song beside his body. On it he had written, "It is hard to die alone . . ."

Few folk are more lonely than those who have a deep worry at the back of their minds. Perhaps they are afraid of the future, or they have a sorrow they can't share. Maybe someone you know is going through an ordeal like that right now.

The answer to the problem of loneliness lies in having a living relationship with the great Comforter and Partner. David wrote, "To the Lord I cry aloud, and he answers me from his holy hill" (Psalm 3:4). Here we see God drawing near to the lost and the lonely. The poet A. Ackley has written:

> No friend on earth could help afford,
> I needed one who was divine,
> And when I met the blessed Lord,
> I knew the help I sought was mine.

It has been said that David Livingstone was one of the loneliest men who ever lived. There is some truth in that, of course. After all, a large part of his life was spent in lonely pioneer missionary work, far from any white folk. He had no choice but to go on for days and weeks and months at a time without a single word to or from an intimate friend. Moreover, Livingstone lived, one might say, on the horizon – always ahead of his time, always planning great tomorrows. Consequently he was aloof from so many of the fussy little unimportant things which fill most people's lives. Pioneers must be solitary people. But Livingstone was never truly lonely. He always had a Companion. All his life his favourite text was, "Lo, I am with you always, even unto the end" (Matthew 28:20). Of that text the great traveller and missionary said, "It is the word of a

Gentleman of the most strict and sacred honour . . . so there's an end of it!"

Jesus was always looking for lonely people. He touched untouchable lepers — men and women who were barred from all human contact. And He talked with despised sinners, showing them that they were important to Him. As His followers, we must be aware of lonely people. Maybe it's a little boy who just can't seem to get the hang of arithmetic and feels ashamed at school. Perhaps it's a woman whose husband ignores her and makes her feel unwanted. It might be a wife with children who has been left by her husband to fend for herself. People like that need a smile, a kind word, a loving deed, an invitation to dinner. Even the smallest kindness, done in Christlike love, can break the chains of loneliness. Jesus reached out to lonely people; we can do the same. The poet Strout has written:

> Jesus, hold my hands so closely
> That Your life and love may flow
> Through my hands outstretched in mercy
> To Your lonely ones below.

If you are lonely, I pray that you may discover God's answer to your suffering. As you find more of His presence and He becomes more real to you, the shadow of loneliness will disappear.

23. "My Peace I Give You . . ."

People today lack peace; they feel disturbed and uncertain. George Bernard Shaw said, "The only thing people are certain about is their uncertainty." Jesus is the only source of true peace. He has been to the Cross to win it for us. He has made "peace through his blood, shed on the cross" (Colossians 1:20). "The punishment that brought us peace was upon him" (Isaiah 53:5). The Bible calls Jesus "the Lord of peace" (2 Thessalonians 3:16) and "the Prince of Peace" (Isaiah 9:6). He said, "Peace I leave with you; my peace I give you. I do not give to you as the world gives. Do not let your hearts be troubled and do not be afraid" (John 14:27).

One day a friend who was filled with doubt and spiritual perplexity came to see the Scottish preacher McLeod Campbell. "Pastor," he said, "you always seem to have peace in your soul. Tell me, how is it that you can always feel that you have such a tight hold on God?" With a smile Campbell exclaimed, "I don't always feel that I have a hold on Him, but, praise the Lord, I know that He always has a hold on me!" This truth can be a great comfort to us in times of trial:

Able to keep! Yes, able to keep,
Though rough the path, all rugged and steep;
Tender the heart that's caring for me,
Mighty the grace, "sufficient for thee".

God holds onto us. We can also have great peace
by holding on to God's promises, which assure us
that we are safe in the heavenly Father's keeping:

Christ's blood makes us safe;
God's Word makes us sure.
And both are the fountain of our peace.

As a Sunday School pupil I was encouraged to
memorise Scripture. There is one verse which I have
never forgotten and which for me has always been
a source of peace and deliverance from fear and
uncertainty. This is it: "I know whom I have
believed, and am convinced that he is able to guard
what I have entrusted to him" (2 Timothy 1:12).

Sometimes our immediate need is peace and quiet.
Any parent will understand what I mean! Malcolm
was a loveable, talkative, energetic five year-old. He
seemed to have boundless energy from morning till
night. There were times when he almost exhausted
his devoted parents. One afternoon the local
minister, who was a friend of the family, called
round. He chatted to Malcolm's parents and after
a while brought the boy into the conversation. "Tell
me, do you say your prayers every night?" he asked
him.

Malcolm stared at the carpet. "Not every night,"
he replied sheepishly.

"Really? And why is that?" asked the minister.

The boy looked up and smiled. "Daddy says them for me," he said. "When he carries me upstairs he often says, 'Well, thank God you'll soon be asleep and the house will be quiet!' And then I say, 'Amen.'"

However, the absence of noise and stress is not necessarily peace. It is in fact an inner quality and a gift from God. Religion cannot give it, money cannot buy it and intellects cannot fathom it. Prime Minister Gladstone used to have this text hanging on the wall of his bedroom: "You will keep in perfect peace him whose mind is steadfast, because he trusts in you" (Isaiah 26:3). He read it each night and morning, and it was the source of the calm strength which sustained him throughout his many years in government.

Turn to Jesus for that abundant, overflowing, rich gift of peace today.

> Oh, the peace my Saviour gives,
> Peace I never knew before;
> For my way has brighter grown
> Since I learned to trust Him more.

24. The Fruit of Righteousness

It has been estimated that since the crucifixion of Christ 8,000 peace treaties have been signed in the world. The rejection of the Gospel offered by Jesus has resulted in mankind being in a state of constant upheaval. Apparently man has not learned his lesson. With blind prejudice he refuses to acknowledge his mistake. He is still searching frantically in other directions for formulas and organisations that may further friendly relations between individuals and nations. In almost every generation there have been prophets who have cried, "Peace, peace!" when there was no peace. Today's topsy-turvy world is so desperate for peace that it will wage war in an attempt to preserve it.

In his heart man craves peace even more than he craves happiness. Often people don't care what sort of peace they obtain – they don't care whether it is true or false, lasting or transient. They will have it at any cost, because they cannot do without it. People are willing to accept any philosophy so long as it gives them a quiet, easygoing life without anxiety or sense of danger. This is in fact the peace of ignorance. Man hopes that somehow or other things will be all right in the end.

But the peace we need today is not the deceitful tranquillity of apathetic neutrality, nor the delusive calm of an armed truce, nor peace at any price, without due regard for righteous principles. We need real peace, and that is an inner quality that comes as a blessing from God and as a result of living according to His standards. Such living brings its inevitable reward. Scripture says, "The fruit of righteousness will be peace; the effect of righteousness will be quietness and confidence for ever" (Isaiah 32:17).

How does this God-given peace of which the Bible speaks work in the lives of those who possess it? It is a calm which was unknown before. The fears that used to fill the soul have died away, like the angry waves which subside after a storm at sea. Tranquillity pervades the heart, just like the sunbeams which break through the opening clouds after a tempest. Agitation and alarm are replaced by serenity and confidence that all is well because the soul is reconciled with God through Christ. Those who receive this gift are forever afterwards grateful that God in His mercy opened their ears to hear the Gospel of peace; their gratitude is all the greater because they have also received the peace of the Gospel.

25. Overcoming Fear

I was conducting a crusade in a small Lincolnshire town. At the meeting I was to lead that night in a local church I was going to show a Billy Graham film. The minister was very nervous indeed, since this was the first evangelistic venture he had ever been involved in. As I was getting the projector ready he kept coming up to me and telling me, "I'm sure something is going to go wrong!" I tried to calm him and assure him that all would go well.

People started arriving, and soon the church was packed out. Again, just as the service was about to start, he came up to me. "What if the projector breaks down half way through the film?" he whined. Finally he started the service. The first hymn was sung and there was a time of prayer. Then I introduced the film and started the projector. All went smoothly for the first five minutes. Then suddenly, just as Billy Graham was getting into full swing with his sermon, the film ground to a halt. The projector had broken down!

The minister turned the lights on and came up the aisle to me, red-faced and embarassed. "I knew this would happen!" he declared.

"It's your fault!" I told him.

"What do you mean?" he asked, amazed.

"Job says, 'That which I feared has come upon me.' You feared, and brought this upon us!"

There was to be no Billy Graham film that night. The people had to make do with me! But God was glorified and many were converted.

This story, although amusing, does illustrate that our fear can bring upon us many things which we would otherwise never have to suffer. Fear is a killer, a destroyer. It brings much misery to millions of lives. The well-known author Philip Toynbee once wrote, "Fear is always the enemy, the deepest of all roots of evil."

Some years ago I led a crusade at the famous Mount Zion Church in Norfolk. A lady who had heard about the miracles of healing which had been happening came for prayer. She was convinced that she had cancer, even though her doctor and a cancer specialist had told her that she did not have it. But she was so sure that she had the disease that she was worrying herself into the grave. I warned her that this fear could bring the very sickness she feared into her body. She would not listen to the Word of God or to medical advice. A year later I heard that she had indeed died of cancer.

Fear itself is often worse than the thing which is feared! Many famous people have confirmed that most of the things they worried about never happened in the end. The comedy actor Bill Maynard, having faced many drastic ups and downs in his life, once remarked in a radio interview that "Fear, which is at the back of worry, is almost always not so much fear of what is happening as fear about what is going to happen."

Most people have secret fears which they don't want anyone to know about. Often they are quite silly and irrational. Lord Roberts, the courageous Field Marshal, was so afraid of cats that he couldn't enter or stay in a room if he knew there was one in it. Some people can't bring themselves to step into a lift; others refuse to fly in aeroplanes. Some people are afraid of birds.

I remember seeing a fascinating television interview of a lion tamer. We saw him at work in a cage full of the most ferocious lions and lionesses. He looked like a tough and fearless man. "Aren't you afraid of anything?" asked the interviewer. "Yes, I am," replied the lion tamer with an embarassed laugh. "It may sound silly, but I'm terrified of mice and spiders!" To think that a man with the courage of a Daniel should be so afraid of such tiny, inoffensive creatures! Interestingly enough, Hitler was also afraid of spiders.

A beady-eyed newspaper reporter once asked me, "Are you ever fearful, Mr Banks?" Doubtless he thought I would boastfully answer that I was never afraid of anything. But he was startled by my answer. "On the first night of a mission I'm petrified!" I said. This worldly-minded journalist and I then went on to have a lengthly discussion.

Yes, I often experience stage fright on first nights. It's the same whether I'm preaching on my own home ground in Chippenham Town Hall, or in one of the churches in Bristol or Exeter, or in the deep jungles of Malaysia and Thailand, or in the Australian

Outback in "Crocodile Dundee" territory, or in the Zulu shanty towns in South Africa, or in New York City, or in Amsterdam or the Hague or Metz or Toulouse . . . I am always nervous during those few minutes before facing so many sick, lost, helpless, broken people. I have preached in cathedrals, on ships, in buses, in house groups, in foootball and rugby stadiums, in dance halls and nightclubs, in some of the largest auditoriums and churches in Europe . . . I feel just as frightened when in front of forty or fifty people in a tiny country church as when I'm about to speak to a crowd of ten or twenty thousand.

I don't think it is a sin to experience such momentary fear, so long as we overcome it. A man of God, in whom I recently confided about this, said to me, "When you lose that feeling of inadequacy you are finished as a preacher. That stage fright shows that you know you are just a man — it shows that you are relying on God alone for your gifts and power and not trying to serve Him in your own strength."

Kathryn Kuhlman was always filled with "trepidation" just before her great monthly rallies in Pittsburgh. Dr Paul Yonggi Cho, Derek Bingham, Ray McAulay, Reinhard Bonnke, Jackie Pullinger and David Watson have all spoken about being afraid sometimes. And yet they have overcome their fears and have turned the world upside down to the glory of God.

I once went to see the grave of Edith Cavell in the close of Norwich Cathedral. She was a courageous nurse in the First World War who was shot by the

Germans for helping Belgian prisoners to escape. While I was there a cathedral guide told me that about seven years ago a small boy from the cathedral school had accidentally knocked over and broken the cross on the grave while he was running about in the close. He could have said nothing about it and got away with it, since no one had seen him. He was afraid of the punishment he might receive. But he was a brave, honest boy, and so with a thumping heart he went and told the headmaster what he had done. A new cross was made for the grave. "That boy will go far," I said to myself. "He will grow up to do what he believes to be right, whatever the cost to himself." Both Edith Cavell and this little boy had fought fear – and won.

Pastor Martin Niemoller, the leader of the German Evangelical Church, was greatly feared and hated by Adolf Hitler. In order to silence him the dictator threw him into prison. Months later he was summoned to appear before a special court. Niemoller was suddenly very afraid – he had no idea what to expect. Was he going to have to face a firing squad? As he was taken along the seemingly endless corridors from his cell to the courtroom he heard one of the guards who accompanied him speaking in a low voice. He was quoting from the Latin version of the Bible used by the German Catholic Church. It was a verse from the Book of Proverbs: "*Nomen Domini turris fortissima . . .*" – "The name of the Lord is a strong tower; the righteous run to it and are safe." We don't know who this man was, but what he said dispelled Niemoller's fears and renewed his confidence in

God's mercy. From that moment he was never afraid again.

The story is told of a passenger on a train who wondered at the calm serenity of a little boy who was sitting alone in the carriage. "Aren't you afraid to be travelling alone?" asked the passenger. The boy looked surprised. "Why should I be afraid," he said, "when my Father is driving the train?" We Christians have a heavenly Father who is "driving the train" of our lives. Trust and faith in Him can deliver us from all fear. Trust in God is the only really effective answer to the problem of fear. Scripture says, "The Lord is my light and my salvation – whom shall I fear? The Lord is the stronghold of my life – of whom shall I be afraid?" (Psalm 27:1).

Let us go forward in our lives, made courageous by our trust in God. Fear need not overcome us, because our Father is always with us. Let us make these words of the Apostle Paul our own: "I am convinced that neither death nor life, neither angels nor demons, neither the present nor the future, nor any powers, neither height nor depth, nor anything else in all creation, will be able to separate us from the love of God that is in Christ Jesus our Lord" (Romans 8:38-39).

26. Why Worry?

If we let it, worry can spoil our lives:

> Worry saddens many a home,
> Shortens many a life;
> Worry keeps a husband glum,
> Makes an edgy wife.
> Worry never calmed a fear,
> Never rights a wrong;
> Worry is the worst thing quite
> That ever came along!

During the Second World War Charles Moran was Winston Churchill's doctor and travelled with him on some arduous and sometimes perilous journeys around the world. He kept a diary of that time, extracts from which were later published in his book, *Winston Churchill: The Struggle for Survival*. He records that on one occasion Churchill asked him, "Is much known about worry, Charles?" Then, without waiting for an answer (which was typical of him!), he went on, "It helps to write down half a dozen things which are worrying me. Two of them, say, disappear; about two, nothing can be done, so it's no use worrying; and two perhaps can be settled." What good advice! Try it.

Sometimes one can find a way of overcoming troubles in the most unexpected manner and in the most unlikely places. A friend of mine was going through a difficult time at work and had to spend long hours at his desk. After several months of this he decided to get away from it all on a fishing weekend in Inverness-shire. One evening he was fishing beside a lovely loch. Suddenly the peace and quiet was shattered by a loud squalling. He raised his binoculars and to his surprise and delight focused on an osprey. Something in the water – a large fish, perhaps – had caught the bird's attention. But each time it swooped towards it, it was mobbed by a flock of seagulls. No matter how the osprey twisted and turned, the gulls still followed it in.

Then the osprey changed its tactics. Slowly it rose in ever-rising spirals. As it gathered height, one by one the squalling seagulls gave up the chase and drifted back down to the lochside. Finally the osprey, now a mere speck in the high, clear air, soared majestically on its own.

As my friend laid aside his binoculars he felt something more than the peace of the evening wash over him. He returned to work a new man, with a new attitude. He was determined that, like the osprey, he would not give in to his worries, but would instead rise above them. And that was exactly what he did.

It's wise not to make too much of our troubles and worries. This amusing verse, written by John Scott of Eday, Orkney, came into my hands recently:

Why Worry?

If you talk about your troubles,
And tell 'em o'er and o'er,
Sure, the world will think you like 'em,
And proceed to give you more!

The late Lord Brabazon of Tara had some very wise advice for those who tend to worry about the future — whether their own or that of the world in which they live. He said in a radio broadcast: "If you can train yourself not to worry, you will have done for yourself more than any doctor can do. The unpleasant things in my life have always happened out of the blue. Meetings and other events I have feared and dreaded like the plague have turned out to be not so bad. Do not hide today's sun behind tomorrow's clouds."

Everything going wrong today?
Everybody mad?
Life depressing as can be?
That is very sad.
What's the use of keeping on
When the fun and thrill are gone?

Just a minute though — perhaps
If tomorrow you
Get up looking for the best,
Trying hard to do
All the good you can . . . and smile,
Life may prove to be worthwhile!

The best advice of all about losing worry and care is to be found in God's Word. "In God I trust; I will not be afraid," writes David (Psalm 56:4). "Cast all your anxiety on him because he cares for you," writes Peter (1 Peter 5:7).

If a trouble hits you hard
You can weep all day,
Moan and groan until you're ill –
Sigh your soul away.
Better far to battle on,
Wear a gallant smile,
Keep on somehow – God knows how –
Mile on weary mile . . .
Till you come home to joy at last,
All your worries long since past!

Yes, that's good advice. Keep soldiering on with God, and remember what His Word says: "Do not be faint-hearted or afraid. . . . For the Lord your God is the one who goes with you" (Deuteronomy 20:3-4).

27. A Few Words

A professor from Yale University was the after-dinner speaker at an academic banquet in England. "As you know," he began, "I come from Yale, so I want to frame my speech around those four letters – 'Y-A-L-E'." His listeners waited eagerly for him to begin.

"The letter 'Y'," he said, "stands for 'Youth'. . ." And he spoke about Youth for fifteen minutes.

"Now 'A'," he said, "is for 'Ambition', the great American virtue . . ." The guests settled down as he spoke for twenty minutes on this subject.

"'L' stands for 'Learning'," he declared, and devoted fifteen minutes to Learning.

"Finally, 'E' is for that great institution, 'Education'. . ." His listeners sank low in their seats as he finished with twenty minutes on Education.

As he sat down he eagerly asked his neighbour, "How did I do?"

"We enjoyed it very much," was the faint reply, "and we are all so glad that you are not from the Massachusetts Institute of Technology!"

Milton said, "The measure of a man is the extent to which he can concentrate on words." It is often said that something worth saying can be expressed in just a few words. I have heard hundreds of preachers all over the world during the forty years since I became a committed Christian. Some I cannot remember, and some I would like to forget! Some of the sermons were as much as two hours long, but some of the best I ever heard were the brief, snappy, sharp ones.

After all, the Lord's Prayer in the Authorised Version has only 65 words in it. The Ten Commandments are expressed in just 297 words, while the American Declaration of Independence comprises just 300 words. However, the Common Market's instructions on the import of caramel products run to some 26,911 words! What a waste of words!

Solomon advises us, "let your words be few" (Ecclesiastes 5:2). James tells us, "Everyone should be quick to listen, slow to speak . . ." (James 1:19). Jesus commanded us not to swear by anything and said, "Simply let your 'Yes' be 'Yes', and your 'No', 'No'; anything beyond this comes from the evil one" (Matthew 5:37). We don't need to use a lot of impressive words to make a promise; a straightforward "Yes" or "No" should suffice.

Some politicians have a reputation for longwindedness – for using several words where one would do. A man was once taken out to a restaurant by a friend. When he had finished his steak and salad he went to the washroom. After washing his hands he went to the hand drier, and as he was about to push the button to make the warm air blow out he noticed with amusement that some joker had written next to it: "Press this button for a tape-recorded message from the Prime Minister." Too many people in politics are full of hot air!

But President Harry Truman was not a bit like that – he had a simple, no-nonsense approach to politics and indeed to life in general. When asked about the rigours of political life, instead of giving a lengthly reply, he would simply say, "If you can't stand the heat, stay out of the kitchen!"

Somebody once asked President Woodrow Wilson how long it would take him to prepare a ten-minute speech. The President replied, "Two weeks." He was then asked how long it would take him to prepare a two-hour speech. "I'm ready now," answered Wilson. So we can see that the art of speaking or writing is not to say a lot but to say a lot in a few words. It is the quality of the words we say that counts, not their *quantity*.

Words are powerful. What we say can be an influence either for good or for evil. Our words should be few, careful and kind. When a family moved into a house they found that a few items had been left in the kitchen by the previous occupants. Pinned to the wall were a calendar, some recipes and this verse:

> Every grouse shakes this house,
> Every grumble makes it crumble,
> But loving words
> Will give it all the strength it needs.

The following comes from what seems a rather unlikely source – *600 Magazine*, a publication for machine tool manufacturers and engineers!

The six most important words in life are: "*I admit I made a mistake.*"

The five most important words in life are: "*You did a good job.*"

The four most important words in life are: "*What is your opinion?*"

The three most important words in life are: "*If you please.*"

The two most important words in life are: "*Thank you.*"

The least important word in life is "*I.*"

Recently I came across a list of nine words which express all that is best and worst in life:

The most bitter word is *Alone*.
The most tragic word is *Unloved*.
The most cruel word is *Revenge*.
The saddest word is *Forgotten*.
The coldest word is *Indifference*.
The warmest word is *Friendship*.
The most beloved word is *Mother*.
The most peaceful word is *Home*.
The most comforting word is *Faith*.

28. My Favourite Hiding Place

I am often away from home for weeks at a time on missions all over the world. It is always a wonderful joy and privilege to preach and to see people saved and healed, and yet sometimes I need to get away from it all. When I am at home I have a hiding place I love to run to. If my wife cannot find me in the house, she knows exactly where I am. I am in the summer house at the end of the patio. There, surrounded by roses, dahlias, begonias and pansies, I lounge in my wicker basket chair and lose myself in a book. There in the sunshine I am a world away from the demands which my work makes upon me, a world away from crowds, phone calls and letters. I love books!

Books enable us to move in a wide world and to possess the rich heritage of mind and spirit which is ours. The playwright Chris Morley said, "When you sell a man a book, you don't sell him twelve ounces of paper and ink and glue – you sell him a whole new life." If we want to escape drabness, boredom and discontent and know colour, excitement and purpose in our lives, we must read. Even in this age, when there are video recorders, satellite TV dishes and computers in so many homes, the old saying still stands: "A room without books is like a body without a soul." Charles Lamb said, "We ought to pray over our books as we say Grace over our meals."

We must make time to read. I feel very concerned when Christians, both young and old, tell me that they have no time for reading. Charles Swindell observed that most successful men and women are well read. It is true that many of the outstanding figures in history had a very high regard for books. Winston Churchill's genius was never more clearly revealed than when he urged architects in Britain's post-war years to include a built-in bookcase in their designs for working-class homes. By the time he was thirteen Harry Truman had read the Bible through three times and had read every single book in his local public library! No wonder he was such a wise President in such a needy time.

Every mother should teach her growing children the value of wholesome books.

> I had a mother who read me lays
> Of ancient and gallant and golden days . . .
> You may have tangible wealth untold:
> Caskets of jewels and coffers of gold:
> Richer than I you can never be —
> I had a mother who read to me.

The adult who can say those words had a truly happy childhood and a good start in life.

John Bunyan, returning in despair from the horrors of the English Civil War, was given a Christian book by someone, and as a result he found Christ. C. S. Lewis was set on the way from atheism to Christian faith when he read the writings of G. K. Chesterton. Chuck Colson was one of the "dirty tricks" politicians involved in the Watergate scandal, but he became a Christian and eventually an evangelist through reading none other than C. S. Lewis! This shows us the value and the power of books.

Some years ago Archbishop Donald Coggan led a campaign by the English churches to get Christian books to the needy Third World. It was called "Feed the Minds" and it was one of the most important crusades ever to take place in this country. How vital it is to provide those who are learning to read with pure, wholesome, happy literature! Many young Christian men from overseas write to me, pleading for books. It has been said of the millions of people in our time who are becoming literate, "Whatsoever is sown in their minds, the world will reap!" How true.

William Caxton set up the first printing press in England in the precincts of Westminster Abbey, and the title page of his first volume recorded this fact. I think it was appropriate that printing in this country should have begun on the site of a place of worship. Today we need to retain that connection between books and worship and to promote and distribute Gospel literature.

I can truly say with Ivor Gurney, the Gloucester-shire poet:

O for a garden to dig in,
And music and books . . .
One could grow happy and whole there . . .

Come, then, and join me in my hiding place!

29. Smile!

When I'm out and about these days I find that I don't see very many people smiling. Even when they're on holiday people seem to do nothing but grumble – about the weather, about the food, and so on. Some time ago I took my children to the pantomime. It was full of good, clean, simple jokes, and I roared with laughter. But I found that I was just about the only one in the audience who was laughing. In fact, some people were staring at me with puzzled frowns. Many people today need to learn how to smile and laugh!

Do you know how to smile and laugh? Test yourself by reading the following stories!

"Mummy, I've got a tummy ache," complained a six year-old little girl. "That's because your stomach is empty," explained her mother. "You'd feel better if you had something in it. You should have eaten your lunch." The next afternoon the vicar called around, and during the conversation he mentioned that he had a headache. "That's because your head's empty," declared the little girl. "You'd feel better if you had something in it!"

An American tourist was visiting one of Britain's quaint country villages and got talking to an old man in the local pub. "And have you lived here all your life, sir?" asked the American. "No, not yet, m'dear," the old man replied.

A minister was delivering his sermon one Sunday morning. "Always jump at the chance to do somebody a good turn," he told his congregation. "You'll never regret it!" Later that day he noticed a small boy trying to reach up to a rather high doorbell. "Let me do it for you, sonny," said the minister, giving the bell a good long ring. "Thanks, mister!" said the youngster, grinning. Then he took to his heels and disappeared around the nearest corner, leaving the minister to face the irate man of the house!

A woman went to the local bank to open an account. She had never even set foot in a bank before and had always kept her money at home. The manager asked her why she had changed her mind about banks. "Well, I've just got married," she replied. "You see, it isn't wise to have all that money lying around when there's a stranger in the house!"

There is a lot of gloom and despondency around these days. We keep hearing awful predictions about the deterioration of the global environment, and there always seem to be numerous trouble spots in the world. In his Pickwick Papers Charles Dickens wrote a description of dismal living which in some ways is strikingly contemporary: ". . . the tired, sad expressions, the careworn faces, the dormant affections, the heartless eye that no longer glints . . ." The prevailing gloom can get us down even if we are Christians. However, we are meant to be "the happiest people on earth", as the writer

of a famous Christian book with that title has said.
David said to God, "you . . . fill me with joy in your
presence, with eternal pleasures at your right hand"
(Psalm 16:11). Knowing God should make us happy
and joyful.

What we need today is a Revival of the Smile!
Among Christian young people during the 1970s a
common motif was a little smiling sun with the
words, "Smile, Jesus loves you!" beneath it. You used
to see this everywhere — on lapels, on car bumpers,
on windows... Once I even saw it on some toilet
paper! Yes, we certainly need a return of the smile...
I like the old rhyme that goes:

Don't dwell on the much that is bad —
Or soon you'll forget how to smile.
Give thanks for the little you've had
Of the joy that makes living worthwhile.
Moans and complaints build walls around you,
Smiles open doorways so friends can come
  through.

This old prayer is so true:

Give me a sense of humour, Lord;
Give the power to see a joke,
To get some happiness from life
And pass it on to other folk.

Someone from Canada gave me this verse:

If you make up your mind today
To look for pleasant things,
For smiles or sunshine, bits of fun,
Surprises fortune brings;

Smile!

If you are slow to find the worst
But quick to spot the best,
You won't be sorry for yourself
But count yourself well blessed.
It's up to you to make today
As sad as sad or bright as a ray!

May you discover the deep heart-warming which Jesus, the "Man of Joy", can give you. Peter described that joy as "inexpressible and glorious" (1 Peter 1:8). Jesus taught men and women in this desperate, unhappy world how to smile. Take to heart the following words – live them, practise them, work at them, express them:

Whatever be your mood – don't be rude.
Whatever comes your way – please be brave.
Whatever cares you know – let them go.
Whatever path you choose – quit the blues.
Whatever be the test – do your best.
Whatever be the strain – don't complain.
To make life more worthwhile, whatever happens
  – smile, smile, smile!

30. A Good Cup of Tea

When I was a young man I spent a while as a Salvation Army officer in the northeast of England. I remember the Geordie people forcing cups of tea on me whenever I visited them! They were such hospitable people – they always seemed to have the kettle on the boil. Any time is the right time for tea.

> I like it at my breaktime,
> By the fireside at night,
> In fact there's no occasion
> When a "cuppa" isn't right!

Do you know that over 200 million cups of tea are drunk every day in the British Isles? The average Briton drinks some 1,650 cups of tea each year. However, over the past five years tea drinking has been on the decline as coffee and wine have gained in popularity. A 1990 survey revealed that now only 45% of the population are regular tea drinkers. The tea industry has been hitting back with large-scale advertising campaigns over the past few years.

Many great men have spoken glowingly of our national beverage. Prime Minister Gladstone said, "If you are cold, tea will warm you; if you are heated it will cool you; if you are depressed it will cheer you; if you are excited it will calm you." Dr Samuel Johnson called himself "a hardened and shameless tea-drinker... who with tea amuses the evening, with tea solaces the midnight, and with tea welcomes the morning." When the poet Coleridge was asked how many cups of tea he drank, he retorted that he did not count it in cups, but in pots! William Booth, the founder of the Salvation Army, used to say, "I like my religion like my tea – *red hot!*"

A group of schoolchildren were on a daytrip to London and were being given tea on the terrace of the House of Commons, which enjoys a superb view of the Thames. "Well, what do you think of all this, then?" the teacher asked them. There was silence for a moment, and then a thirteen year-old lad piped up, "The tea's a bit strong, Miss!" There he was, amidst all that fascinating architecture and history, in the very heart of British democracy, and all he could think about was his cup of tea. A true Englishman!

With a cup of tea we can cheer people and make them feel welcome. David Hope has written this verse:

> Her window faces north; her room
> Is winter-dark and bare;
> Small is her fire; old are her bones –
> She's known a load of care.
> But folk with troubles like a cup
> Of tea with her – she cheers them up!

Glenda Moore of Dunscroft, Yorkshire, has written this lovely poem:

My grandmother's cottage,
I fondly recall,
Had masses of roses
On its outside wall.
While deep in the centre,
Beneath the old thatch,
A warm welcome awaited
The lift of the latch!

Brass warming-pans,
Her lace wedding gown,
The old cherished hat
With the white satin crown.
The cottage, and Grandma,
I remember them still,
And her warm cup of tea
At the foot of the hill.

Over a cup of tea I have seen many a problem
solved, many a need met, many a prayer of
repentance prayed and many a grave situation
turned into triumph as it has been committed to
the Lord our God. Over a cup of tea I have seen
prayer allay fears, despair disappear and misery turn
to hope. I have seen shattered lives rebuilt, broken
hearts consoled, dismal, bored souls given a new
glimmer of light, and lost people enter into a new
land of milk, honey and grapes. I have seen those
in the spiritual gutter raised to newness of life. A
chat over a cup of tea can be a time of great spiritual
value. The next time you do it, don't just natter
about anything but speak words of God, faith, love,
courage and certainty. I heard of one pastor in
Cornwall who banned tea from his church! What

a pity — I've seen so many miracles take place over a cup of tea.

Recently an insurance salesman visited me, not to sell me a policy but to ask me for prayer and counsel. My wife got the kettle on and soon we were in deep discussion over a cup of steaming tea. Tears came to his eyes as he told me his troubles. Before long I was able to lead him to Christ and pray for his healing. God touched him that day! Today he is fit and well and full of thanks to God.

Recently, when I was crusading in France, a young Chinese businessman invited me to his home for afternoon tea. I was willing to travel the forty miles there for the sake of a good cup of tea! When I arrived he and his wife opened up to me and told me that their marriage was in trouble. The man was having an affair with another woman and didn't know what to do about the situation. I prayed, the Spirit of God came on him and caused him to break down. He repented sincerely, asking his wife to take him back. They started their married life again, this time with God in the central place in their hearts and in their home. I'll not forget that cup of tea and what God did that afternoon. The latest I have heard is that they are united, happy, working for God and going forward together.

We shouldn't think of the subject of drinking as earthly, carnal and unspiritual. On the contrary, drinking can have great spiritual significance. Jesus drank with a Samaritan woman at a well. He talked with her and led her to salvation, and afterwards she became a flaming evangelist. The stories of Abraham, Elijah, Ezra, Esther and Nehemiah all speak of the blessings, fellowship and joy which drinking together can bring (of course, they didn't have tea in those days – they would have drunk wine or water).

Why not invite that neighbour or business associate or workman or dustman or paper boy or milkman or insurance salesman in to share a cup of tea with you? You will find that you will have opportunities to speak to them about the Master you love and about His miracle-working power which can change their lives.

Now, I'm going to put the kettle on and enjoy a nice "cuppa". Won't you join me?

31. Man's Deepest Need

Forgiveness – it is not only the most beautiful word in the English language, but also the most powerful experience which anyone can enjoy. Horace Bushnell said, "Forgiveness is man's deepest need and highest achievement." The head of a large mental home in Britain – someone who does not claim to be a Christian – said recently, "I could send half of my patients home tomorrow, fully cured, if I could assure them of forgiveness." Forgiveness has great power to heal the mind. The character Macbeth in Shakespeare's play of that name was tormented by guilt. He longed to be able to "pluck from memory a rooted sorrow, raze out the written troubles of the brain"; he longed for "some sweet antidote" which would free man from his guilt, "that perilous stuff which weighs upon the heart".

The Hebrew and Greek words for "to forgive" literally mean "to put away" or "to let go" or "to send away forever". To forgive means to "send away" someone's sins. As Thomas Adams put it, true forgiveness happens when "sins are so remitted, as if they had never been committed". Adam and Eve, the parents of mankind, through their disobedience lost the special communion and fellowship which they had with God, and so we, their descendents, are in the same predicament. We can only be restored to fellowship with God when our sins are *sent away*, when we have God's forgiveness. Gaining that forgiveness, through faith in Jesus Christ, is the only way for us to get right with God the Father, the only way to true and lasting peace and joy and the only way to escape the judgement of God on the Last Day.

Since we have been forgiven by God, we must forgive our fellow men. Jesus said, "Forgive, and you will be forgiven" (Luke 6:37). Forgiveness is a central part of the Christian life. Paul encouraged the Ephesian Christians to "Be kind and compassionate to one another, forgiving each other, just as in Christ God forgave you" (Ephesians 4:32).

> God's way is the best –
> It is the way of forgiveness,
> It is the way the Master went;
> Should not the servant tread it still?

Mrs Billy Graham was once asked what made a happy married life. Her answer was, "Two good forgivers!" Forgiveness is vital for strong, harmonious family life.

In Pemain, a town in America, there is a road called Split Rock Road. It is named after an extraordinary natural phenomenon. A tiny seed once took root in a small crevice in a large boulder. It grew steadily and gained strength. Finally the plant was stronger than the boulder and split it in two. Then there were just the two halves of the rock with a tree growing between them. This can be seen as a picture of the power of forgiveness. Though it seems weak and insignificant it can eventually break apart the biggest and toughest of problems and obstacles.

During my thirty-five year-long career as a Gospel preacher I have seen forgiveness bring about amazing transformations in people's lives. I have seen it happen all over Britain and indeed all over the world – in the islands of the Pacific, in the streets of Moscow, in the slums of Birkenhead, in the terraced streets of Belfast, in the quiet fishing villages around John O' Groats and Land's End. People are released from all kinds of bondages when they forgive those who have wronged them in the past. Then the darkness of yesterday gives way to the sunshine of a bright new tomorrow.

A while ago a lady rang me at my office in Chippenham to tell me the wonderful thing the Lord had done in her life. At one time she had been so sick and in such pain that she had had to use sticks to get around. She had been prayed for a great deal, but to no avail. Then one day the Lord showed her that she had an unforgiving heart. She repented of this and started to forgive the people who had wronged her. Ever since that time two years ago she has never had to use the sticks!

A doctor who was treating a patient for nervousness and insomnia discovered that he felt great resentment towards his mother-in-law. The doctor recommended a month's stay in a recuperation centre, well away from her. That was good advice, but not quite good enough. At the end of the month the man came home feeling much better, but within days all his previous symptoms started up again. He needed to pray for his mother-in-law the prayer which Jesus prayed on the Cross: "Father, forgive them, for they do not know what they are doing" (Luke 23:34).

Alice and Jane were sisters living in a certain town in southern England. Twenty years ago they had had a disagreement over something and had not talked to each other since. Each was unwilling to forgive the other. They even passed each other in the street without speaking! Then one day Jane heard that Alice was dying, so she went across town to see her. She came and sat silently at the end of the bed, and Alice stared at her coldly. Finally Alice said, "The doctor says I have not long to live. If he's right I forgive you. If I recover from this things stay as they are." What a small, unforgiving heart!

Are you a forgiving person? A readiness to forgive is one of the marks of those who are right with God.

> Be the first to make it up,
> Your differences to end.
> What does it matter who's to blame?
> Forgive, forget, be friends.
> Mistaken pride is out of place,
> So start again anew.
> There must be one to take the lead,
> Could that one not be you?

32. Close the Gates Behind You

History is full of examples of how forgiveness has transformed and ennobled people's lives. Some years ago I was reading the life of Abraham Lincoln, that great idealistic American leader. I wanted to know what made him tick, what his secret was. One of the things about him which impressed me most of all was that, in Emerson's words, "His heart was as great as the world, but there was no room in it to hold the memory of a wrong." That was the secret of his greatness.

Lloyd George used to tell the true story of a doctor who had been greatly respected around Criccieth in Caernarvon. When he lay dying he was visited by the local minister, who asked him whether there was any last word or message he would like to give. There was a long pause, and then the old doctor painfully raised himself on one elbow. "No," he said – and there was another pause – "except this. Through life I have always closed the gates behind me." He had always been willing to forgive.

Stanley Baldwin was a very unhappy man towards the end of his life. His wife had died and a lot of people seemed to be blaming him for the outbreak of the Second World War. He was very surprised to receive an invitation to lunch from Prime Minister Winston Churchill. Baldwin had treated Churchill badly during the latter's years in the political wilderness, but "Winnie" was a great forgiver. He even went so far as to confide in Baldwin about some of the most secret questions of the war and to ask him for his opinion. Perhaps Churchill didn't really need Baldwin's advice, but with his intuitive sympathy he knew that it would please a lonely and ailing old man.

After the German invasion of Belgium during the last war a group of Belgian teenagers were praying the Lord's Prayer together in a church. After the words, "Forgive us our trespasses" they paused, wondering if they could bring themselves to finish the sentence. Could they forgive the Germans, who had ruined their country? As they thought about this they heard a voice behind them say, "As we forgive those who trespass against us." They turned round and were astonished to see that the speaker was the King of Belgium himself. He had lost his country, but he had not lost his soul.

During the Second World War the Dutch Christian Corrie ten Boom was imprisoned in a Nazi concentration camp for harbouring Jews. She suffered terribly there and almost died. After the war she happened to meet again a man who had been one of the guards at the camp. A terrible desire for revenge welled up within her as he stood there before her. She almost went and hit him, but by God's grace she controlled herself. In her heart she yielded to Christ and offered the man her hand and her love. What a testimony! The power of God within her enabled her to turn the other cheek in loving forgiveness. Jesus commanded us, "Love your enemies, do good to those who hate you, bless those who curse you, pray for those who ill-treat you" (Luke 6:27). Peter said, "Do not repay evil with evil or insult with insult, but with blessing" (1 Peter 3:9).

33. Little Kindnesses

Scripture tells us that we should "Be kind and compassionate to one another" (Ephesians 4:32). And yet, sadly, the "milk of human kindness" is in short supply today. What a difference to life kindness makes!

I once saw a gravestone in a pretty churchyard in the Surrey countryside which simply declared, "He was so thoughtful in little things." What an admirable epitaph. Here was a man who was remembered for his small kindnesses. The poet Wordsworth said that the "best portion of a good man's life" was "his little nameless, unremembered acts of kindness".

Dr Wilfred Grenfell was a remarkable pioneer missionary who brought the Gospel and medical help to many people in Labrador. He had a plaque on the wall of one of his surgeries bearing some words about Jesus, whom he sought to follow:

> He did kind things so kindly –
> it seemed his heart's delight
> to make so many happy
> from morning until night.

The Queen Mother is a kind, gracious lady with an

understanding heart. She was once in Leeds to confer the freedom of the city on HMS *Ark Royal*. Some of the ship's crew were lined up for her to review, and she stopped and spoke to one of the men. But he couldn't answer her because he had a cold and had lost his voice! So the Queen Mum delved into her handbag and found him a throat lozenge. Homely touches like that endear her to us all.

This verse is very apt:

> We need a lot of clever folk
> To do big things today.
> We need inspired leaders who
> Can show us all the way . . .
> And kindly folk who seem to be
> Concerned about just you and me!

A chauffeur who was new to his job was told to go to the railway station to pick up his boss, whom he had not yet met. He asked for a description and was told, "When you see a tall, strongly built man helping somebody with something – that will be him." Arriving at the station, the chauffeur noticed a man helping a disabled woman off the train. Sure enough, this turned out to be his boss. A kind heart always shows, even in a crowd.

I like this prayer:

> Endow me, Lord, with strength to face
> Life's biggest griefs and ills;
> And give me, also, grace to bear
> Life's little cares and chills.
> Oh, make me patient, loving, kind . . .

When you visit the sleepy little village of Cavendish

in Suffolk, all seems sunshine and peace. There are brightly painted thatched cottages all around the sloping village green, and the parish church looks over the tranquil scene. But one of the houses there has a remarkable story to tell. After the last war a lady named Sue Ryder, who lived in the village, turned her own home into a refuge for concentration camp victims. She did a marvellous job, caring for them as they recovered from their appalling sufferings. She went on to found the Sue Ryder Foundation, which to this day still cares for suffering, homeless, destitute people. The house in Cavendish is still its headquarters. There is an old hourglass in the church in Cavendish which reminds worshippers and visitors that the hours of life are passing. Sue Ryder, through her kindness towards those who were suffering, shows us that it is possible to fill each hour with purpose, effort, sacrifice and love.

Someone has written,

> If ever you've a little thought,
> an urge to do a friendly act –
> don't stifle it, but go ahead,
> and turn that impulse into fact.
> A kindness done to someone sad
> will make your own heart twice as glad.

The greatest of all Norwegian musicians was undoubtedly Edvard Grieg. This gifted son of Norway had a hard fight for recognition. He was scorned by many who ought to have known better. His gallant fight went on until Liszt, the famous Hungarian composer, gave Grieg a kind word of praise and declared that his Piano Concerto deserved immortality. This gave the young composer the courage to persevere until fame came to him.

Every day we influence those around us for good or for ill. Indifference or criticism can wound or depress them. But kindness, patience and encouragement can bring out the best in them.

Emily Dickinson, the celebrated American poetess, beautifully expressed the value of kindness:

> If I can stop one heart from breaking,
> I shall not live in vain;
> If I can ease one life the aching,
> Or cool one pain,
> Or help one fainting robin
> Unto his nest again,
> I shall not live in vain.

When he went out for walks the Duke of Wellington often used to chat to a ten year-old local lad whom he knew. One day he noticed that the boy was not his usual cheerful self. The Duke asked him what was wrong. "Well, sir, I have to go back to boarding school tomorrow, and there is no one to look after my pet frog." The Duke replied, "Cheer up! I don't know much about frogs, but I will see to him for you until you get back. Bring him to my house." And the boy did! That's a trivial incident, perhaps, but it shows that the Iron Duke had a kind heart.

The Australian poet Henry Lawson wrote:

> The main thing for the present is just only to be
> kind –

You can always hear the scandal but you don't
    know what's behind.
Take what friends can give in friendship and pass
    on what you can get,
And while jokes and kindly words can cheer, your
    life's not wasted yet —
Never fret!

34. More Little Kindnesses

I remember an old tramp who used to call at my home every summer when I was a boy. He had a long beard and ragged clothes and carried all his possessions in a handkerchief on the end of a stick. Mother would never let him in the house, but he was allowed to sit on a chair outside on the garden path. She would give him a cup of tea and a large slice of freshly baked cake. He was always very courteous and would have a friendly chat with us. Then he would don his cap, thank my mother very politely and be on his way. The next year he would be back. Helping and caring is good.

The newspaper reporter John Hargreaves was once out driving in his car. Suddenly the engine coughed, spluttered and died. First of all a motorist coming in the opposite direction flashed his lights angrily to tell John to get out of the way. So he pushed his car until it was just off the road. Next, a churchgoing acquaintance saw his predicament and passed on laughing. Then a man came and told him to "shift it or else", since the car was now on private land. Finally a worker from a nearby mill arrived and helped John to push the car to the mill's car park. John had never seen the man before and has never seen him since, but he now understands, as never before, the old story of the Good Samaritan and Christ's teaching about practical kindness.

> Plan a little kindness,
> Plot a friendly plot,
> Make a bit of sunshine
> In some gloomy spot.
> That's the way to cheer up
> Folk who're feeling sad . . .
> Odd that it is sure to
> Make your own heart glad!

During the last war a lady in Perth had a Polish doctor billeted in her house. He had come to Britain as a medical officer in the Polish Army and had managed to bring his elder son with him. He knew that he was more fortunate than many of his countrymen, and yet his heart was heavy. For eighteen months he stayed with the Scottish lady. When his son got leave he came to stay with them. Then the doctor's health began to give way. Eventually he passed on and was laid to rest in Perth. The lady often thought about his family but she never heard from them – until recently. One day, there on her doorstep stood the doctor's son, and with him were his mother and his younger brother. Together they had made a pilgrimage to Perth to see the doctor's grave. Now they were calling on the Scottish lady to thank her sincerely for what she had done for him all those years ago. People from all over the world respond to kindness.

Life's a sort of boomerang:
Knock somebody out,
Sooner or later you'll catch a blow
that you cannot doubt.

Life's a sort of boomerang:
Kindnesses you do
Bless a lot of people, then
Circle back to you.

In Neil Munro's novel, *The Shoes of Fortune*, one of the characters is carried home to die after being wounded in a fight in which he had been trying to protect a child. These were his last words: "Be good, be simple, be kind. 'Tis all I know . . . Fifty years to learn it, and I might have found it in my mother's lap."

When I was a boy the local newsagent's was run by an elderly couple who were well known in the district. The man was a cheery, red-faced, kindly, loveable character. The lady was more stern and severe and was a real disciplinarian with us youngsters. We would often hear her say, "I don't know what the modern youth are coming to!" When things were quiet they used to take it in turns to serve in the shop. We boys used to peep inside to see who was serving, and if it was Mr Smith we would go in for a bag of our favourite slab toffee. But not if Mrs Smith was serving! You see, the toffee had to be broken off the slab with a hammer, and if a bit too much went into the bag she would remove some of it until the weight was exactly right! But with her husband it was different. Even if the bag was much too heavy he would quickly tie it up and cheerfully toss it across to us.

Jesus, talking about blessing, said "A good measure, pressed down, shaken together and running over, will be poured into your lap" (Luke 6:38). How much happier we could make other people, and how much happier we ourselves would be, if we were always on the lookout for that little bit extra we could do for someone. After forty-five years I still remember old Mr Smith's kindness!

35. A Helping Hand

Recently my wife and I were passing through London on the Underground, on our way to catch a plane to Germany. We had to change stations three times, and amidst the mad, rushing crowds of the capital we found it quite a struggle with all our luggage. However, two people offered us help. The first was an Arab man who kindly carried a heavy case for us and even came back down some steep stairs to get another one. The other was a scruffily dressed West Indian young man. Both showed us great kindness. This set me thinking about the gift of helping others. Often people ask how I received the gift of healing. Sometimes they ask me to pray that they will receive it, or the gift of working miracles. But it's not often that I'm asked to pray that someone might have the gift of helping others (1 Corinthians 12:28)!

Jesus taught that His followers had to help others. He commended the woman who gave Him water at the well, and the greatest story He told was about the good Samaritan who went out of his way to help another. The writer of Hebrews encourages people to welcome strangers into their homes, adding that by so doing they might be entertaining angels without knowing it (Hebrews 13:2). Solomon wrote, "I know that there is nothing better for men than to be happy and do good while they live" (Ecclesiastes 3:12). A songwriter has written, "God has no hands but our hands." That's not quite correct, but there's a lot of truth in it. God has largely limited Himself to using people as His means for bringing blessing and help to other people. As the hymn says, "Take my hands and let them move at the impulse of thy love . . ."

Sometimes it doesn't cost us much to help someone, and it makes a big difference to them:

It takes very little to help folk along –
A word may bring comfort in grief,
A smile or some kind help to the harassed or worn
Can cheer a hard day past belief.
It takes very little – but have we the wit
To see where it's needed a lot,
The heart quick to share,
And the hand which is there,
And are we ready to give what we've got?

A minister in British Columbia had a parish consisting largely of islands on the province's coast. On one occasion he was holding a service in the cabin of his small steamer for a gathering of loggers and miners. He had just opened his Bible when a cry came from the shore that a man had been seriously injured. Immediately the minister ordered the crew to take the boat to the scene of the accident, and the whole congregation sped on their way on their errand of mercy. One of the loggers – a huge, tough, bearded man – afterwards declared, "That was the best sermon I ever heard in my life!" To help someone in need is perhaps the best way to recommend God to those who don't know Him.

> How sad that folk should suffer pain,
> That gallant hearts should break,
> That grim misfortune now and then
> Kind folk should overtake.
> How sad . . . and yet how good to know
> Some friend will understand,
> And where there's need will run at once
> To give a helping hand.

An man was once at York Bus Station, waiting in a queue for his bus to come in. He noticed a poorly dressed elderly woman shuffling dejectedly away from the queue. He went to her and asked if there was anything he could do for her. She told him that she had wanted to go to Leeds but had discovered that she didn't have enough money for the fare. He had no spare money to give her. What could he do? He led her over to the very long queue and asked each person in it to give her two pennies. Everyone gladly obliged and in no time the old lady had her fare to Leeds – and more!

Someone has written:

> Pause a minute – you will find
> You have the time to help mankind;
> A cheerful word, a friendly smile
> Makes their life, and yours, worthwhile.

One day a middle-aged woman walked into the office of a debt collection agency. "I hear," she said, "that one of your men has been to see a neighbour

of mine about a debt she owes. I want to pay it."
She took a fifty pound note out of her purse, handed
it over and walked out beaming. Why did she do
it? Because she admired her neighbour so much and
realised that the debt was not her fault. The young
woman was a good wife and mother who, despite
her present difficulties, had never missed giving five
pounds a week to her own mother, who was a
widow. Imagine her joy when she received the letter
telling her that someone had paid the debt for her!

A Christian man may be the most brilliant scientist
or the finest musician or the greatest statesman. He
may even be a notable preacher, but if he has
forgotten the personal touch and the little kindnesses
and no longer puts individual people's needs first,
then in reality he has become a backslider. We all
need to live the life of Jesus, practising simple
kindness and living to help others. Do all your good,
kind, loving acts now, before it is too late, while you
and your loved ones, your friends and acquaintances
and the strangers you meet are still alive.

Jesus said, "You are my friends if you do what
I command" (John 15:14). And what is it that He
wants us to do? He wants us to be friends to others.
Be a friend to them now; don't leave it until it is too
late. One wife wrote these regret-filled words:

> Ah me, the kindly happy things
> I could so easily have done
> For him – my very life – before
> His race was run.
>
> Too late, too late – the chance has gone
> For precious words or deeds of love . . .

A Helping Hand

Make a covenant with God today and rededicate youself to lifting, healing and changing our friendship-starved world – our lost, sad, lonely, forlorn generation. You might find it helpful to say the words of the verse below:

I promise . . .

> To help another on life's way,
> To smile and chase a frown away,
> To right a fault, reveal the good,
> To love my neighbour as I should,
> To comfort someone who is sad,
> To make a lonely person glad,
> To share my joys and blessings, too,
> This will I try each day to do.

36. Temptation

During my boyhood I lived in Chippenham, a small country town in Wiltshire. When May came around each year my friends and I would creep into the Paddocks, a grove of horse chestnut and hazlenut trees. There we would illicitly gather conkers for playing with and walnuts and hazelnuts for eating. We used to have marvellous conker competitions. One would bore a hole through the centre of a conker with a meat skewer, push some string through it and tie a knot on the bottom. Then each competitor would have three attempts to crack his opponent's conker. The first to succeed won the game. The old trick of hardening your conkers in front of a coal fire was strictly forbidden!

We boys knew that it was wrong to go into the Paddocks and take the nuts, but it was just too tempting for us. What a pleasure it was to go and get the first and toughest of the conkers and to pick up some delicious walnuts and hazels on the way! But as soon as the owner, Mr Awdry (a solicitor who later became our local MP), appeared on the scene — red-faced, waving a stick and rushing across the Paddocks towards us — we all disappeared rapidly! We used to get a severe rebuke from Mum or a hiding from Dad if they found out about it!

The story is frequently told of the little boy who went into an orchard one warm September day. He sat directly under one of the trees and looked up at the great big, rosy apples, licking his lips and thinking about how juicy and tasty they must be. The owner of the orchard found him there. "And what do you think you're up to?" he asked. "Are you going to steal some of my apples?" "I'm trying not to!" the boy replied.

Oscar Wilde once remarked, "The only way to deal with temptation is to give in to it." That is very poor advice. Giving in to temptation is destructive and in the end disastrous. We Christians must resist temptation. The secret of this is to keep well away from the things, people and pleasures that tempt us. The alternative is guilt, loss of self-respect, further moral weakness and a life full of problems.

When we become Christians Christ Himself comes and lives in us. He gives us the strength to resist temptation. Scripture says, "God . . . will not let you be tempted beyond what you can bear. But when you are tempted, he will also provide a way out so that you can stand up under it" (1 Corinthians 10:13). By the grace of God we can resist the temptations of life, whether they be the more obvious ones such as sexual sin, tax evasion, dishonesty, bad temper, jealousy, pride and so forth, or the more subtle ones like trying to please men rather than God. Paul wrote, "For sin shall not be your master, because you are not under law, but under grace" (Romans 6:14).

A man came to a minister one day and said to him, "I was at the meeting you led last night. At the end of it I did just what you asked me to do – I took Christ into my life by faith. I didn't feel any different at the time. But at work the next day I found to my amazement that all the temptations I normally suffer from didn't bother me any more. I just didn't want to do any of those things anymore. They were uninteresting and repellent to me. Then I realised that something had happened in my life. Christ was in me, and He had given me a new strength."

Another man who had just become a Christian gave the following testimony: "I was a bad-tempered man. If anyone crossed me, I flew into a rage. But the day after I became a Christian it was different. Someone wronged me, and I felt the familiar anger rising up inside me. But I sensed straight away that this was a wrong reaction and so I resisted it. That's the first time I've ever done that!" Who told the man that flying into a rage was wrong? Christ Himself. The new life was at work within him. If we have Christ in our hearts, we have the power to overcome temptation. As Paul wrote, "I can do everything through him who gives me strength" (Philippians 4:13).

37. The Watchdog in the Heart

Immanuel Kant said, "There are two things that have filled me with awe: the starry heavens above, and conscience in the breast of man." The human conscience is invisible and mystifying, and yet it is very real. In ancient times there was a legend of a magic ring which pressed painfully upon the finger of its wearer whenever an evil thought passed through his mind or he was tempted to do an evil deed. Our conscience is just like that ring. When we try to do wrong, it presses painfully upon our soul. When we do what is right it gives us peace within our hearts.

When Charles XI of France lay on his deathbed he cried out in remorse and fear, "If only I had spared the weak and the little children!" He was referring to the bloodthirsty murder of thousands of Huguenot Christians which had been committed under his orders. He could not rid his conscience of the guilt of that infamous act.

One man in the USA who had been cheating the income tax authorities for years became cut to the heart about it. Trying to appease the voice of his conscience, he wrote an anonymous letter: "I have defrauded your department. . . . I am sending back a large amount. If I find that I still don't have peace of mind after this I will return the rest of what I owe you." But of course, this sort of attitude isn't good enough! Like Zacchaeus, we must return everything that we have dishonestly gained. There can be no half-measures when we are dealing with our conscience. We will never get complete forgiveness and peace until we put everything right.

In a certain town there was a great revival in which many people were converted to Christ and convicted of their sin. The local post office sold out of postal orders, because there was suddenly such a great demand for them. Many of the people whose consciences had been touched by the revival wanted to repay their bad debts or to give back money which they had taken dishonestly. It was a wonderful visitation of God.

There are many instances in Scripture of people being troubled by their consciences. In Genesis Joseph's brothers, who had been thrown into prison in Egypt, said to one another, "Surely we are being punished because of our brother. We saw how distressed he was when he pleaded with us for his life, but we would not listen; that's why this distress has come upon us" (Genesis 42:21). Just after King Ahab had gained possession of Naboth's vineyard by murdering its owner, the prophet Elijah went to him. "So you have found me, my enemy!" he said to Elijah (1 Kings 21:20). And yet just a short time before this they had parted as friends. It was Ahab's troubled conscience which caused him to call the holy man his enemy. King Belshazzar was so convicted of his sin by the mysterious hand that

wrote upon the wall that "his face turned pale and
. . . his knees knocked together and his legs gave
way" (Daniel 5:6). To the Pharisees who wanted to
stone the woman caught in adultery, Jesus said, "If
any of you is without sin, let him be the first to throw
a stone at her." Their consciences were pricked and
they "began to go away one at a time, the older ones
first" (John 8:7, 9). In the Book of Acts Felix, the
Roman governor of Caesarea, stood trembling
before the prisoner Paul because he was the slave
of a guilty conscience (Acts 24:25). Shakespeare
wisely declared, "Conscience doth make cowards of
us all."

Lord Byron wrote:

> Why should not conscience have vacation
> As well as other courts of the nation,
> Have equal power to adjourn,
> Appoint appearance and return?

But we should never try to make our conscience have
a holiday. We shouldn't try to make it sleep, because
it is a vital watchdog. We get into grave trouble if
we ignore it. The Bible tells us that one's conscience
can become "seared" (1 Timothy 4:2), "corrupted"
(Titus 1:15), "guilty" (Hebrews 10:22) and "weak"
(1 Corinthians 8:7). It encourages us to have a "good
conscience" (1 Timothy 1:5) which is alive and
sensitive.

When people deliberately ignore their consciences
they often try to change, dilute or compromise moral
values to suit their own lowered standards. For
instance, in George Orwell's *Animal Farm* Squealer
the "dictator" pig secretly changes the wording of

one of the animals' "seven commandments" to suit the downward trend of the pigs' morality. He alters the command, "No animal shall kill another animal" to "No animal shall kill another animal without cause".

We should not kill, sear, deaden or disregard our conscience. Paul said, "I strive always to keep my conscience clear before God and man" (Acts 24:16). We should listen to and obey our conscience and we should respond to the Holy Spirit as He convicts us.

38. Good Character

A man who worked as a clerk for a certain company had applied for a better job with another firm. He was interviewed by its manager. "Do you have any references?" he enquired.

"Yes, sir," replied the clerk. "I have two. One from the minister of my church, and one from the Superintendent of the Sunday School I attended when I was a boy."

"Fine," answered the manager, "but do you have any references from people who know you on weekdays?"

It's comparatively easy to give a good impression on a Sunday, but it's more difficult in the nitty-gritty of workaday life!

Good character isn't as highly prized as it used to be, and yet it is as important as ever. In today's fickle, immoral, empty, shallow, skin-deep society we need people who are reliable, honest, sincere, respected and transparent.

Joseph Maxwell of Hemel Hempstead had spent forty-two years of his life as a teacher – and not only in the usual sort of schools, but in borstals and approved schools too. There is much that I could tell you about him and about the many ways in which he helped thousands of boys to face manhood. But I think all of this is summed up in the inscription engraved on the silver salver which was presented to him by his former pupils on his retirement:

> Respected as a man,
> Admired as a teacher,
> Cherished as a friend,
> And loved as a companion.

Could any man, in laying down his life's work, ask for a finer or more noble tribute? As Scripture says, "A good name is rather to be chosen than great riches" (Proverbs 22:1).

William McKinley became President of the USA in 1843. Soon after entering office he had to choose an ambassador to be sent abroad. Two candidates came instantly to mind. Both were fine men. McKinley couldn't decide which would be better for the job. Then he recalled an incident which had occurred years before. He had boarded a street car, and at the front had been one of the two men whom he now had in mind. An old washerwoman had then boarded, but as there had been no vacant seat, she had had to stand, swaying to and fro. The man had continued to sit while, right next to him, the woman had struggled to keep her balance. Eventually McKinley himself had given up his seat for her. Remembering this, the President gave the job to the other of the two men. He was looking for a man who displayed thoughtfulness, consideration, kindness and manners in private life as well as in his work. He believed that someone who was going to represent the American people ought to be a person of good character.

In a similar way we are God's ambassadors in the world. May we live up to His high standard; may our lives display the highest morals, manners, values and conduct, so commending Him to a dead, groping, empty shambles of a world. Paul said that we must "bear fruit in every good work . . . think on whatever is of good repute . . . not grow weary of doing good . . . be rich in good works . . ." (Colossians 1:10, Philippians 4:8, 2 Thessalonians 3:13, 1 Timothy 6:8, all NASB). May we Christians be known as people of good character!

39. Are You a True Friend?

Recently a tragic accident in the city of Bath in the West Country claimed the lives of two men in their early twenties. They had been born on the same day in the same hospital ward. They had grown up together. They had gone to the same school and had joined the same sports club. One had been the best man at the other's wedding, and the married man had anticipated returning the favour when his friend got married. Late one winter's night the car they were driving in skidded and hit a tree. The two men died together and were even buried next to each other. Theirs had been a friendship which had endured all through their lives.

The motto of one of the finest regiments in the British Army is "And they were not divided". The words are taken from the biblical story of David and Jonathan, who had an undying friendship. The value of friendship cannot be overestimated.

Some years ago a well-known writer dedicated one of his books to another distinguished scribe with these words: "To my friend, Dr William Barclay, one of the blessed who give without remembering and receive without forgetting." I wonder if anyone could say the same of you or I. Are you a true friend?

Are You a True Friend?

Of course, there are many different definitions of a friend. Here is a good one which I have heard: "someone who knows the worst about you but continues to believe the best of you". If you have three or four friends like that you are rich indeed. William Penn, the Quaker who ventured from Buckinghamshire to found the American state of Pennsylvania, said: "A true friend assists readily, adventures boldly, takes all patiently, defends courageously and continues a friend unchangingly. The covetous, the angry, the proud, the jealous, the talkative cannot but make ill friends."

I like these sayings about friendship:

"The best time to make friends is before you need them."

"The best way to keep friendships from breaking is not to drop them."

"A true friend laughs at your stories even when they're not so good, and sympathises with your troubles even when they're not so bad."

"When you've made a fool of yourself, a real friend doesn't believe you've done a permanent job."

"Friendship is like a bank account – you can't draw upon it without making deposits."

There is a story about a certain king who was at war with a neighbouring king. His cabinet were fed up with the whole affair, as the war had practically ruined their country financially. So they asked the king, in the event of his being victorious, to destroy his enemies utterly and completely. The king considered their request and consented to it.

However, when victory was gained the king, to the surprise of his cabinet, gave the defeated nation a huge tract of land. His cabinet were indignant, and asked him why he had done this. The king smiled. "I have kept my promise," he said. "I have destroyed my enemies utterly. They are now my best friends."

The other day I read the classic story of Prince Alexis, heir to the throne of Russia. Knowing that one day he would rule over his father's kingdom, he determined to get to know his people before he became Tsar. So he set off to tour the country with a retinue of courtiers and soldiers to impress his future subjects. But wherever he went the people fled and hid in terror and fear.

Bitterly disappointed, Alexis consulted a wise old friend, who told him he had gone about it the wrong way. "First win their trust and love," he advised, "and then you will win their allegiance." So Alexis trained as a physician and then went humbly among the people, compassionately tending to their needs and healing them. When he came to the throne the people willingly gave him their loyalty, since by being a friend to them he had won their hearts and trust.

I have never actually seen the old film, *The Bride of Frankenstein*, but I have read that in it Frankenstein, played by Boris Karloff, tries to get the manmade monster to talk. He can only get it to say two phrases: "Food good!" and "You friend!" Even Frankenstein's monster had one friend! But, you know, there are many human beings who have lived all their lives without finding one true friend.

Are You a True Friend?

I have seen loneliness in all its shapes and forms. How it can affect a person! Sometimes there isn't a thing I or anyone else can do about it because of five little words which almost guarantee loneliness: "I keep myself to myself." I recently received a letter from someone who had heard their neighbour say these words. "I know she's very lonely," said the letter, "and I wish I'd had the courage to tell her that friendship is a two-way thing, and that you have to go halfway to meet it."

We do well to remember these words:

> I went out to find a friend; a friend I could not see.
> I went out to be a friend; and friends just flocked to me.

Sir James Simpson, the outstanding scientist who discovered the anaesthetic properties of chloroform, wrote before he died: "In Christ you will find a . . . companion, a friend, a brother who loves you with a greater love than a human heart can conceive." Proverbs says God is "a friend who sticks closer than a brother". Jesus said, "You are my friends if you do what I command" (John 15:14). It is amazing, staggering and wonderful to discover the personal friendship of God.

I like these lines by J. Small:

> I've found a friend, oh such a friend,
> So kind and true and tender,
> So wise a counsellor and guide,
> So mighty a defender . . .
> I am his forever.

He was speaking of none other than our glorious

Lord and Saviour, Jesus! He wants to be our friend, and He wants us to be friends to others. Let us follow the example set by our Master Jesus and be a true "friend who sticks closer than a brother".

40. A Second Chance

Thomas Edison, the famous inventor, had just finished making the very first perfect light bulb. After years of wearying experiment and painstaking work, he had finally got it just right. This was what he had dreamed of achieving.

He handed the bulb to one of his employees, a boy named Jimmy Price, telling him to take it upstairs. Jimmy went off to do Edison's bidding. Suddenly the inventor heard a smashing noise. The bulb had slipped through Jimmy's fingers and had broken on the floor!

We can well imagine Edison's sense of loss and how angry he must have been. And yet he said nothing. Instead he went back to his workbench and began to build another bulb from scratch. Several days later he completed it. It was then that he did a big thing — a very big thing. With a smile he handed the new bulb to Jimmy. "Careful, now!" was all he said. Not only did he forgive Jimmy, but he gave him a second chance too.

John Mark, the writer of Mark's Gospel, was also given a second chance. As a young lad (perhaps as young as fifteen) he had accompanied the Apostle Paul on his first missionary journey. This was probably the first time he had been away from home for a long period, and the first time he had been involved in a big evangelistic outreach. For some reason which is unknown to us he couldn't cope with it all and left Paul when he greatly needed help and companions and loyal workers. However, many years later Paul sent for John Mark and gave him a second chance to work with him. He then had a successful ministry, and went on to write his Gospel. It is a book full of miracles and hope and has been published in nearly every language in the world, and is read by countless millions of people every day of every year. That just goes to show us that even someone who fails and needs to be given a second chance can go on to achieve great things for God!

Sometimes we may need a second chance in life not because we have failed but because some tragedy or other has laid us low. About forty years ago the Rev John Paterson visited a member of his congregation whose beloved little daughter had just died. The man showed him a picture of her. "This little girl used to run and meet me every night," he said bitterly. "Now she's dead. When she was sick I prayed harder than I'd ever prayed before, but she still died." He turned and faced Paterson with tears in his eyes. "Don't ever ask me to come to church again!"

Paterson knew that nothing he could say then could heal the man's sorrow, and with sadness he said goodbye and left.

A few days later tragedy struck the minister's own home. His week-old little son died. His birth had filled Paterson with joy, but now that joy was forever shattered. And yet through the dark days that followed the minister kept his faith in God. Less than a fortnight after he had last been there, he returned to the house of the man who had lost his daughter, conscious that he could now help him in a way that would have been impossible before, since he had now suffered the same loss. When the man answered the door Paterson held out his hand. He simply said, "George, I still believe."

The next Sunday Paterson was in his pulpit and the other man was in his pew again.

There was once a businessman who as the result of an accident became paralysed from the waist down. All his life he had believed and trusted in God. Now, weary and resentful, he asked his minister bitterly, "What's my faith worth now? Nothing!"

For a moment the minister didn't reply. Then he said, "I'm deeply sorry for you and I know how you must feel about your faith. But before you throw it away, ask yourself if doing that will make you better. Will it solve your problem? Will you be any happier without faith in God?"

The man had been expecting to hear words of comfort, which he would have rejected. Instead he had been challenged, and he knew that what the minister had said was true. He came to the realisation that all was not lost and that while there is breath there is life, and while there is life there is hope. He pulled himself together and lived many more years, succeeding in his business and being a great blessing to the people in his church.

So if you have failed in some way or you have been devastated by some tragedy in your life, take heart.

I have seen thousands of people who had no hope, who were waiting for the undertaker, being met by the "Uptaker". Jesus meets us in our times of need and lifts us up, saves us, changes us, answers our prayers and gives us a new start in life.

41. Be a Dreamer

Hans Christian Andersen spent his whole life writing stories that made children happy. Very often his inspiration came from real life. The beautiful and moving tale, *The Little Match Seller* was based on the experience of his unfortunate mother. As a child she used to be sent out to beg, and she would be ashamed and afraid to go home empty-handed. Andersen's story of the ugly duckling which becomes a beautiful swan has given encouragement to countless youngsters who have seen themselves as ugly ducklings in their own families. It is true that we need practical people to get the daily work done, but how dull life would be without dreamers like Hans Andersen! In his autobiography he wrote, "Life itself is the most wonderful fairy tale."

A friend of mine who likes climbing was asked recently to accompany a lame botanist up a mountain, at the top of which he hoped to find a particularly rare species of wild flower. Knowing the dangers and difficulties of such a climb, my friend had some doubts about the wisdom of the idea, but in the end he agreed to go. So the twosome set out to climb up to the dangerous gully where the flower might be found. Because the botanist's only thoughts were of the flower he longed for, he was oblivious to danger and did things which no experienced climber would have dared to do. He climbed up steeps which they would have pronounced unclimbable and unwittingly caused his companion untold anxiety. At last he reached the gully and cried out with delight as he saw that the precious flower was there in abundance. In some mysterious way his singlemindedness had kept him safe. Regardless of the risk, he had pressed on to fulfil his dream. People often achieve success by just forgetting about the difficulties in their path and keeping their eyes on their goal.

Someone has written:

> The dream seems quite impossible,
> Far, far too big for you;
> You know it's quite beyond you,
> And a job you'll never do.
> But have a go — and here's one thing
> That thousands have proved true —
> You can do the impossible!

There was once a sickly boy who dreamed of being a writer. He wanted to record for posterity what life was like in his generation. But he received no encouragement, and his dream sometimes seemed impossible to him. The poor little fellow was blind in one eye and had a limp, and yet he had to make his own way home from school. Feeling concerned for him, his schoolmistress one day decided to follow him at a discreet distance to make sure that no harm came to him on his way home. However, eventually he noticed that she was following him and told her furiously that he did not need any help. Some seventy years later, when he was buried in Westminster Abbey, all that was needed to mark his grave was a simple stone bearing the inscription, "Samuel Johnson". The weak, diseased boy had through sheer determination fulfilled his dream and become the world's greatest diarist.

> Make straight your back, your shoulders square,
> It only takes a minute,
> But that's the way to face a day
> That has some challenge in it.
> Press on with hope, your head held high;
> Even though dark clouds block out your sky
> Your dream will one dark day be reached
> If kept within your heart's own niche.

Some dreams are not happy ones, but are full of foreboding. I once stood at the grave of someone who had had such a dream. It was that of Eric Blair, who was better known as George Orwell, the writer of *Nineteen Eighty-Four* and *Animal Farm*. His bleak predictions about a society of darkness and totalitarianism brought a new word into the English language — "Orwellianism". I visited the grave (which is at Sutton Courtenay in Berkshire) on a beautiful, bright day in May. The cemetery was full of buttercups and rhododendrons. To me it seemed strange to be looking at Orwell's gravestone amidst such lovely surroundings. Thank God that the Christian dream does not take us into darkness and chains but into light and liberty.

Karl Marx said, "The philosophers interpret the world. The point, however, is to change it. . . . You have a world to win!" Even the Communists have a vision and a hope. We Christians have infinitely more cause for hope than they, because we have Christ! We must throw everything to the wind in full abandonment to the Holy Spirit and catch the splendid vision which He wants to give us. We must renounce cynical pessimism, which is dishonouring to God and incompatible with the Christian faith, and replace it with the confident realism which we find in the Bible. George Bernard Shaw said, "You see things as they are, and ask 'Why?' But I dream things that never were, and ask 'Why not?'" That must be our attitude – we must dream big dreams and pray and work towards them. We must have a large vision of how the power of God can change our lives, the lives of those around us and the life of the world. We must make Christ supreme in our lives; we must let Him fill our hearts and minds and inspire our visions, desires and goals. We must live by Christ, with Christ, on Christ and in Christ. We must be ambitious and adventurous for God and His Kingdom. When our dreams are at last realised we will cry out as David did, "O Lord, our Lord, how majestic is your name in all the earth!" (Psalm 8:1).

42. Self-control

Peter the Great of Russia put his finger on a very important truth when he said, "I can govern my people, but how can I govern myself?" When the Apostle Paul was before the proud Roman governor Felix he spoke about "righteousness, self-control and the judgement to come" (Acts 24:25), and that made Felix afraid. He knew himself to be a man who lived an unbridled life. The same has been true of many of the great men of the past – the kings, the philosophers, the poets. They tasted a certain glory, but that glory was mixed with grief and canker. Consequently their glory brought them no satisfaction, as many of them were ready to confess. Alexander could conquer the armies of Persia but he could not conquer his own passions. Napoleon Bonaparte made the whole of Europe his own, but he could not subdue his own ambitions. In the end these led him to exile and disillusionment.

The Bible teaches us that the man who conquers himself is far greater than the man who conquers vast territories. The wise King Solomon declared, "Better a patient man than a warrior, a man who controls his temper than one who takes a city"

(Proverbs 16:32). Achieving self-control is surely the greatest of all pursuits. This is a far loftier ambition than the desire to possess any crown or sceptre. For to overcome self is in fact to overcome the world and to know perfect freedom.

What a paradox man is! He can control the beasts of the field and design huge, complicated and powerful machines which can take him to the planets. He expects to be able to control the weather and harness the sun's energy before long. He sees a fantastic future ahead of him – a wonderful new world that boggles the imagination, a utopia better than our greatest dreams. And yet self will dog his footsteps and torment him. If man's future goals are ever realised, self will still be with him, robbing him of the enjoyment of his achievements. Self is man's number one enemy, and this is why the highest priority should be given to bringing it under subjection.

The Word of God warns us again and again about letting one's self get out of control. Job said, "I made a covenant with my eyes not to look lustfully at a girl" (31:1). King David said, "I will watch my ways and keep my tongue from sin; I will put a muzzle on my mouth" (Psalm 39:1). Another psalmist said, "I have kept my feet from every evil path so that I might obey your word" (Psalm 119:101). The Apostle Paul said, "I beat my body and make it my slave" (1 Corinthians 9:27).

A marriage guidance counsellor invited young couples to go and see him and discuss their difficulties. He asked them all to write down on a piece of paper what they thought was their main problem. One fellow wrote just one word on his slip of paper — the word "Me." If we would all be as honest as him we would be halfway to solving our problems.

But here is the vital question: How can we deal with the "Me"? What is the answer? Paul shows us the way in his letter to the Galatian church. He says that when we yield our lives to God unreservedly and let Christ fill us with the Holy Spirit, we can then attain the desired result. He says, "the fruit of the Spirit is . . . self-control" (Galatians 5:22). If we are fully yielded to God, the Holy Spirit, who dwells within us, will deal with every evil force and make our lives into a harmonious whole.

People often attempt to achieve this in their own strength. Indeed, at times it appears that they have succeeded in subduing their passions and bridling their spirits, but then the inner conflict suddenly flares up again and the battle rages with even greater force. They discover that what they thought was victory was just a false truce, and that the old enemy is as powerful as ever. But when the Spirit of God is in control of our lives He gives us the victory, the war is over, and our souls enjoy peace. A poet has expressed this victory thus: "Make me a captive, Lord, and then I shall be free."

The New Testament tells us several times that true Christians are "bondslaves" to Christ. This actually means coming into an inheritance, receiving power and sharing Christ's authority.

When this happens to a man he knows what Paul calls "the glorious freedom of the children of God" (Romans 8:21). He is no longer a servant of sin but a servant of God and becomes what the Bible calls an "overcomer".

43. Be a Good Listener

Halfway through his highly effective preaching career the Rev John Watson was suddenly attacked by lung trouble and was obliged to rest for six months. In particular he had to rest his voice – a considerable trial for someone accustomed to using his voice in the service of others. He and his wife took a holiday in Europe and Egypt and worked out a strategy so that Watson could remain silent during train journeys without seeming rude to the other passengers. If the fellow traveller who wanted to talk to him was a German, Watson would listen and from time to time gently clear his throat. When the traveller was a Frenchman, he would listen and at the end smile and give a one-word assent. In the case of English-speaking travellers, who were naturally delighted to find someone with whom they could talk, it was more difficult to keep to just a few words, but again Watson did his best to simply listen. He found that through all this listening he learned a great deal and gave many people pleasure and relief. He "gathered the harvest of a quiet tongue" and performed a ministry of silence.

Everyone loves a good listener! People are waiting for someone who will hear them. Jack Ashley, the

MP for Stoke on Trent, was at the start of his career in politics when he suddenly became profoundly deaf. He thought of resigning, but, encouraged by his wife and friends, was able to overcome this disaster. He said in later life, "Human affection and kindness are not plumbed to their depths without crisis. . . . It gave me knowledge of others, of despair, of hope . . . a greater understanding of others." It made him a listener and gave him a compassion for other people and a concern about their needs. He became a listener not with his ears but with his heart and mind.

Listening to others is so important. It it tremendously helpful to them, and it can bless us too. Some years ago I came across this verse:

I listened to a friend distraught with grief,
And the reading of that letter
Warmed my heart beyond belief.
Though my own heart had its sorrow,
Yet I shared another's load;
Lo, a miracle! That sorrow
Led us to a sunny road.

"Go placidly amid the noise and haste, and remember what peace there may be in silence. As far as possible, without surrender, be on good terms with all persons. Speak your truth quietly and clearly; and listen to others, even the dull and ignorant. They, too, have their story." These words, dated 1692, were written on a piece of paper found in Old Saint Paul's Church in Baltimore. Nearly three hundred years later we can still appreciate their wisdom.

Be a Good Listener

God is the greatest listener of all. On her first time at Sunday School a little girl heard the chorus which begins with the words:

> God is still on the throne
> And he will remember his own . . .

The next day the girl's mother heard her singing the song over and over again, but she hadn't got the words quite right. She was singing, "God is still on the phone"! But in a way the little girl was right, wasn't she? Perhaps some of us would pray more often if we remembered that God is always there and far more ready to listen to us than we are to speak to Him. Every hour of every day God hears millions of broken, crying people praying with every kind of request.

Jesus was a good listener. He always had time to listen to people, to understand them. He was such a good listener because He always listened attentively to the voice of His Father.

An elderly man who was hard of hearing was once telling a friend about his marvellous new hearing aid. He said it was very expensive but well worth the cost, as it had given him perfect hearing. "What make is it?" enquired the friend. "Half past five," replied the man! Rather like him, some of us are not so good at hearing others as we think we are. We listen with our ears but not with our hearts. Let's become perfect listeners, like Jesus was.

In our office in Chippenham my colleagues and I receive hundreds of letters every week. They come from despairing people with sad, problem-filled minds. They want someone to listen to them, and so they write to us. The gift of being a good listener is rare and very precious. Let's stop talking and give ear to someone worse off than we are. This will be a tonic of inestimable value to them.

44. Let's Get Away from It All

The writer Indra Derbi says in one of her books, "Modern man works in a hurry, and eats in a hurry and rests in a hurry." How right she is! So many people today have lost all sense of tranquility and quietness. The restlessness of the world has got into their minds and hearts. An expression one often hears is, "He's a hard man to get hold of." We think of being too busy as a good thing, while in fact it is a bad thing. Every day we see the modern world's excessive busyness. People drive their cars too fast, in a hurry to get somewhere just a few minutes sooner. When an aeroplane lands at an airport there is a mad rush for the doors even before the engines have stopped! When I travel by air I just take my time and wait for the rush to finish. I then disembark and join my fellow passengers, who are now waiting impatiently at the baggage claiming area. All that rushing doesn't gain them anything!

There are times when most of us, oppressed by the rush and turmoil of life, feel the need to "get away from it all" for a while. This feeling isn't something new. The Roman emperor Marcus Aurelius, who lived in the second century after Christ, wrote a famous book called the *Meditations*.

In it he said, "Men seek retreats for themselves, houses in the country, seashores and mountains . . . but nowhere, either with more quiet or more freedom from trouble does a man retire than into his own soul." Wise words indeed! Today, as in the times of Marcus Aurelius, it is possible to get away from it all without going on a long journey to some remote place. Instead we can withdraw into ourselves in quietness, prayer and meditation. This was just what Jesus meant when He said, "When you pray, go into your room, close the door and pray to your Father, who is unseen" (Matthew 6:6).

Jesus knew the value and importance of times of quiet alone with God the Father. The Gospels give us glimpses of his private prayer life in a number of places: "Jesus often withdrew to lonely places and prayed" (Luke 5:16); "Very early in the morning, while it was still dark, Jesus got up, left the house and went off to a solitary place, where he prayed" (Mark 1:35); "he went up into the hills by himself to pray" (Matthew 14:23).

If in repose and quiet we concentrate on things which are good and true and beautiful, and *above all on Jesus Himself*, then it will be possible for us to exclude from our minds much that disturbs and annoys us. This is not mere escapism – rather, it is a personal, inner victory over outward circumstances. As the old hymn says, "There is a place of quiet rest *near to the heart of God*."

The words of this famous hymn well express our need of God's peace:

Take from our souls the strain and stress
And let our ordered lives confess
The beauty of thy peace.

Peter said that we should have "the unfading beauty of a gentle and quiet spirit, which is of great worth in God's sight" (1 Peter 3:4). David said, "he leads me beside quiet waters, he restores my soul" (Psalm 23:2). Bernard of Clairvaux said, "Waiting [resting] on God is the work that beats all other work." "O Lord, slow me down!" was a prayer often prayed by the famous preacher, Dr Sangster. Sir Walter Raleigh used to pray, "Give me a scallop shell of quiet." The great Scottish writer, Robert Louis Stevenson, prayed, "Thank you, O God, for courage . . . and a quiet mind."

It is said that one of Beethoven's greatest melodies was composed in Vienna while Napoleon was bombarding the city. Amidst the din of shot and shell the deaf musician was conscious only of the inner harmony which was engrossing him.

One Sunday night I listened in to a church service on the radio. The singing was wonderful – I had never heard anything like it. And yet the service almost didn't take place at all. It was the night of a very bad storm. During the broadcast the lights in the church failed for a time. And yet the very challenge of the darkness, thunder and lightning seemed to inspire the congregation. They sang as they had never sung before. And when they came to sing the hymn, "Be still, my soul", it was as if the words, "Be still . . . the winds and waves still know his voice" were meant for them especially.

Let us turn away from the manifold distractions, the chafing pressure and the mad, scrambling, panting feverishness of modern life! Let us remember to keep the world's tension and rush out of our hearts and to let God's peace and quiet in.

45. The Secret of True Happiness

A child once wrote these words on a wall in a Nazi death camp:

> From tomorrow on I shall be sad,
> From tomorrow on.
> Not today. Today I will be glad.
> And every day, no matter how bitter it may be,
> I shall say:
> From tomorrow on I shall be sad,
> Not today.

That poor child had to fight hard to get even the tiniest scrap of happiness. But many people today who have never experienced such appalling suffering and who lead ordinary lives find happiness hard to attain. Someone has called it "the most elusive quality of our age".

The famous comedian Tony Hancock, who made millions laugh with his TV programme *Hancock's Half Hour*, eventually committed suicide in Australia. His last words were, "true happiness is impossible to find". His tragic case was rather like that of the man who consulted a doctor about his deep unhappiness and dissatisfaction with life. The doctor advised him to go and see a certain clown who could make even the most miserable people happy. The man replied, "I am that clown!"

One evening I went to the theatre to see a play based on C. S. Lewis' Narnia stories. As I looked around the audience I saw many strained faces and very few happy ones. And yet at the end of the show, during which we had been taken through Lewis' wonderful imaginary world, there were smiles all over the place and not a sad face to be seen anywhere. People need to be cheered up – they want joy and happiness.

Happiness, of course, is not to be found in material things. Jesus said, "a man's life does not consist in the abundance of his possessions" (Luke 12:15). A fabled king learned this lesson. He was very unhappy and asked a wise man how he could find happiness. "Find the happiest man in your kingdom, borrow his shirt and wear it," was the wise man's reply. So the king searched throughout his kingdom and finally found a poor woodcutter who seemed supremely happy. The king explained his reason for visiting him and then asked the man for his shirt. But he was so poor that he didn't even own a shirt!

We can be happy despite the most adverse of circumstances. In 1942 George was injured while serving aboard a minesweeper and was brought home paralysed from the waist down. The paralysis was permanent, and he spent most of the rest of his life in hospital and often had severe back pain. However, he was sustained by his faith in God and remained a happy man despite his disablity. He had a fine voice and often used to sing his troubles away.

The Secret of True Happiness

Sometimes he would have an organ pulled to his bedside and would play it lying on his stomach, leading the ward in the singing of a hymn. Recently his long years of suffering came to an end, and with his passing a triumphant song of faith and courage has ended. But I am sure it will linger on in many a heart. George taught us that real happiness is found through faith in God.

The Bible tells us about many unhappy men who became disillusioned with life. King Saul, Jonah, Pilate, Demas and the Prodigal Son are some prime examples. But the Bible also gives us the recipe for true happiness. It tells us, "blessed [or happy] is he who trusts in the Lord" (Proverbs 16:20). To trust in God is to *lean on Him entirely*.

Years ago a missionary was translating the Bible into a native language and came to that very text. He was having problems finding a word for "trusts". Then one of the native preachers came in to talk with him and asked if he could put his feet up on a chair. The expression which he used literally meant "to rest all one's weight here". The missionary jumped out of his seat with excitement. "That's it!" he cried. "That's the word I'm looking for!" And so he used it in his translation.

That is what trusting God means — to rest all your weight on Him, to hand over your whole life to Him, to trust Him as Lord, King and Saviour. Such trust is the secret of deep, perfect happiness.

46. Thank You!

My son and I had just finished a round of golf. I wasn't used to doing so much walking and felt a little out of breath. I hadn't had much practice in recent years, so I had taken a thrashing that afternoon. We started to make our way off the course together. "Well, that was a great game," said my son. "Thanks for giving me your time, Dad." That little "thankyou" warmed my heart. It let me know that my son, although in his twenties, still appreciated spending time with me. I had enjoyed our afternoon together, but his thanks made it even better for me.

Some years ago I went on a gruelling but thrilling nine-week-long preaching tour of Australia and New Zealand. The last part of the campaign was in Queensland. By the end of the ninth week I was exhausted, so my organiser in Queensland thought it would be a good idea if my last meeting there was a small one. He arranged a meeting at a place called Crows Nest, a small village "out in the sticks". I hadn't preached in such a small place since my early days as an evangelist. The church had only fourteen members, but the warmth of their welcome was overwhelming. My wife Lilian and I felt bowled over by their love and hospitality. "We don't know how many people will come to the meeting," they confessed apologetically. "We hope you won't be disappointed." I told Lilian, "You know, even if no one comes to this meeting it will have been more than worthwhile coming here, just for the sake of encouraging these faithful Christians!" Yes, they certainly had faith. They were lifting up the banner of witness in an out-of-the-way frontier town.

What a surprise I had when I got to the church at 7.00 p.m., half an hour before the start of the meeting. The building was full to bursting point! It was the biggest crowd the church had ever seen. Eighteen people responded to my message and came forward to commit themselves to Jesus or to rededicate their lives to Him. Many were healed. One man was able to throw aside his crutches and dance! Never before had such a thing been seen in that village.

At the end of the evening there were tears in the Christians' eyes – tears of gratitude. They appreciated it so much that we had come so far to give them our time and fellowship. But I felt just as thankful as they did. "Well, thank you for letting me come!" I said. I had learned so much from these simple country people – things I would not have learned in a large meeting attended by thousands.

It's so important to express our thanks to people. Have you ever thought of catching the newspaper boy and just saying, "Thanks", or thanking the train driver for bringing the train safely to its destination? Do you ever thank the waitress in the cafe or the assistant in the shop? Do you ever write to thank the people on television who provide you with wholesome entertainment?

Thankfulness doesn't cost us anything. It costs nothing

- to say "Thank you" or "That's fine";
- to shake hands warmly;
- to give someone a pat on the back;
- to listen to someone else's story, even if you've heard it before;
- to tell a child a story or bandage his knee or give him a kiss at bedtime or make funny faces;
- to be polite and considerate;
- to crack a joke;
- to give a little sympathy;
- to carry a smiling face and a kindly spirit around;
- to look for the best;
- to write a letter of thanks to the nurses once you're out of hospital;
- to thank the minister for his sermon after a church service.

Saying "Thanks" is so easy to do, and it makes such a difference to those whom we thank.

47. Give Thanks to God

When I was a small lad I used to go to the children's meetings run by the Salvation Army. They used to teach us to be thankful to God. We used to sing the song:

> We thank You, Lord, for blessings
> You give us on our way;
> May we for these be grateful
> And praise you every day.

We have so much to thank God for:

> Sunshine, birdsong, friends and neighbours,
> Lots of things to do;
> Health and strength and fun and laughter –
> These belong to you!
>
> Aches and pains and heaps of worries,
> Griefs that hurt a lot . . .
> Thank the Lord for all the troubles
> You just haven't got!

A small boy was in a certain hospital when it was visited by a duchess. She was shown around the wards and eventually came to the boy's bed. "Hello, sonny," she said cheerily.

"Hello, Missis," he replied.

The sister was embarassed. "You shouldn't say that," she told him. "You should say, 'Your Grace'."

At once the boy piped up, "For what we are about to receive may the Lord may us truly thankful."

We should be like that little boy – always ready to give thanks to God!

In the early 1900s a policeman walking his beat in Chicago noticed a man standing in front of a little mission hall. The officer thought he was behaving rather strangely. Thinking he might be drunk or ill, he approached him. The man's eyes were closed, so the policeman nudged him. "What's the matter, Mac? Are you sick?" The man looked up at him and smiled. "No, sir, I'm not sick," he said. "I was converted right here in this mission hall. I never pass this way without taking the opportunity, if possible, to stand quietly for a moment and whisper a prayer of thanksgiving." The policeman smiled with understanding and gave him a hearty handshake. The man who had been praying was Billy Sunday, a well-known evangelist.

A certain man had the job of driving patients to a mental hospital. Having taken someone there one day, he was walking to his car when he heard someone calling out, "Hey, you!" The voice came from an upper floor of the hospital. Looking up, the man called back, "Are you speaking to me?" "Yes," came the reply. "I want to ask you a question. Have you ever thanked God that you have a healthy mind?" Later the driver told his friends, "I suddenly realised that even though I had been bringing people to that hospital for fifteen years, I had never once thanked God that I had a good mind!"

It's good to count your blessings:

> Count your joys instead of your woes.
> Count your friends instead of your foes.
> Count your courage instead of your fears.
> Count your laughs instead of your tears.
> Count your health instead of your wealth.
> Count on God instead of yourself.

A poet has written:

> If I sit down and start to count the worries I
>   have got,
> I'll never smile again because of ills I've such
>   a lot;
> But goodness me, I've blessings too – I count
>   them by the score,
> I have indeed no end of things to thank the good
>   Lord for!

When I see the first rose of summer I am always reminded of something which was once said by a wise old gardener: "A lot of folk grumble because God put thorns on roses, but I think it's better to thank Him for putting roses on thorns." To me, that sums up an attitude to life that can make many a dull day brighter.

I am touched by the story of the little girl who went to school one Monday morning looking brighter than usual. "Did you have a nice weekend?" her teacher asked. "Oh, yes, Miss – very nice," was the reply. "Daddy wasn't drunk, and he was nice to us all." That's the sort of story which makes us think twice, isn't it? She was so grateful for a blessing which most of us would take for granted.

Prime Minister Stanley Baldwin received some disastrous news one day during a Cabinet meeting. It was a bad day for the government and for the country. He looked his ministers in the eye and pointed to a bowl of roses on the table and said, "Plunge your faces into those fresh flowers and thank God." In the midst of difficulties he could still see hope, beauty and thanksgiving.

Henry Allford's life was touched by tragedy from beginning to end. His mother died in giving birth to him. His two sons were his pride and joy, but both of them died while still children. Yet not a day went by when he did not thank God for the blessings that had been granted him – the love of his wife, the joy of his home life and the beauty of the world around him. One day, having walked home through the fields at harvest time, he sat down and began to write what he felt in his heart. When he had finished, what was to become one of the Church's finest harvest hymns lay on his desk: "Come, ye thankful people, come, raise the song of harvest-home". This is a song of thanksgiving which is heard in almost every church in the land.

Two farmers in the far north of Scotland were out one day in some of the worst weather which their part of the world had seen for some time. Hail lashed their faces and the wind stabbed at them like a knife. The snow and ice on the ground made the going very hard. They were trudging up a steep hill, and the climb seemed to go on for ever. Darkness was fast approaching and they were still a long way from shelter.

"It's cruel, David," one of them declared, "mortal cruel! I canna stand much more of this hail and wind — it makes me that short o' breath, man! I tell ye, it couldna be worse weather, and you and I couldna have things worse!"

"Oh," replied David, "it could be worse for me. Suppose I had all this to face with a complaining companion!"

The other man scowled, and the two walked on doggedly and silently till they reached their journey's end.

We don't need more to be thankful for; we need to be more thankful for what we have. It is good to keep a thankful spirit at all times. Let a thankful heart take you through this day. Are you learning to offer the sacrifice of thanksgiving to God continually? R. Adams wrote:

> As endless as God's blessings are,
> So should my praises be
> For all His daily goodness
> That flows unceasingly!

Let Jesus be the object of your gratitude! As the chorus says,

> Worthy is Christ,
> Worthy is He of our praise;
> Magnify Him with thanksgiving,
> Gladly your voice to Him raise.

48. Confidence

"No confidence – that's my problem, Mr Banks!" said the man, tears welling up in his eyes. "I don't have so much as a pennyworth of confidence in myself!" People have often told me that sort of thing. And yet many times in the Bible we read of people who had no confidence in themselves being anointed with a God-given confidence. This was true of Elijah, Jonah, Isaiah, Peter, John Mark and many others.

Under the law of the Roman Empire a soldier who deserted his legion had to have the little finger of his right hand chopped off. As a young man John Mark went on a missionary journey with the Apostle Paul but deserted him in his hour of need. Later he returned to Paul's side and became a faithful missionary, even writing one of the four Gospels. There is a story dating from the early Church that he cut his own little finger off as a permanent reminder to himself never to lose confidence again. Tradition suggests that he was known in the Church as *Kolobo-Dactylus*, which means "Maimed-in-the-Finger".

I was recently trying to help someone who had a desperate feeling of being inferior. There is no doubt that many people are not getting the best out of life because they feel like this. They are afraid of themselves and afraid of other people and of what they think about them. But God answered all our quibbling about our own worth when He allowed His Son, Jesus Christ, to die on the Cross. We were worth so much to God that He was willing to sacrifice even His Son in order to buy us back from sin and death.

We need to remember that the initiative is always with God. When Adam and Eve, having eaten the fruit of the tree of the knowledge of good and evil, were hiding from God in the garden, He came looking for them, calling, "Where are you?" This clearly shows that God is forever approaching man. Of course, the climax of His seeking after man was Jesus' coming into the world. And it was to timid men, who were constantly worried about their lives and their relationships, that He said, "You did not choose me, but I chose you" (John 15:16).

This is the only solid basis for our hope. Remember that it is the same for everyone. You are not worth something to God because you serve His Church or because you are good or clever or because you give money or say your prayers. You are worth something because He has chosen you and you belong to Him.

Perhaps you have let this fear about yourself, this awful feeling of inferiority, burden your personality. Perhaps you have got to the stage where the only happiness that you have is to be miserable. You need at this very moment an injection of the confidence that only Jesus Christ can give through His Spirit.

You need it, and He will give it to you. God's Word tells us that He "is able to do immeasurably more than all we ask or imagine, according to his power that is at work within us" (Ephesians 3:20).

Years ago the late Dr W. E. Sangster published a book entitled *He is Able*. Its theme was the power and gracious willingness of Christ our Lord to help us with life's everyday problems. Some of the chapter headings were as follows: "When worn with sickness – He is able!"; "When in loneliness – He is able!"; "When evil thoughts molest – He is able!"; "When I find it hard to pray – He is able!" In all of life's circumstances – in every problem we meet, no matter how difficult the task, no matter how heavy the burden, no matter how sharp the pain – Christ is able and willing to help us.

You see, Christian confidence and hope is not a matter of having the right kind of temperament. It is a question of entrusting yourself to God. He is able to keep all that we have entrusted to Him (2 Timothy 1:12); He is able to build us up (Acts 20:32); He is able to make all grace abound towards us (2 Corinthians 9:8); He is able to keep us from falling (Jude 24); and He is able to help us when we are tempted (Hebrews 2:18). He is able! What confidence and hope and promises of grace are to be found in these passages! No matter what the problem or need or pain or loss you face today, take heart, for Christ your Lord has the power to help and comfort and sustain you. The Apostle John says, "This is the assurance [confidence] that we have in approaching God: that if we ask anything according to his will, he hears us" (1 John 5:14).

Confidence

Stop rushing about, stop doing things, and really pause for a few minutes and consider the fact that Jesus loves you in spite of everything you have been or have not been. There will never come a time when His love for you will break down. You may reject His love, you may shake your grubby little fist in His face and say, "Leave me alone!" – but He will still follow you, He will still be with you.

49. One Day at a Time

Many famous writers have written about time. Isaac Watts, the great hymn writer, said, "Time is an ever-rolling stream bearing all her sons away." Emerson wrote, "The surest poison is time." T. E. Lawrence of Arabia wrote, "Time is a vale of tears and sadness." But the poet Browning declared joyfully, "My times are in His hands."

How often people say, "I haven't the time." I hear these words most often when I'm engaged in evangelism. I remember that when as a young preacher I used to knock on people's doors, inviting them to church, they often used to say, "I haven't the time." The old hymn goes:

> Time for business, time for pleasure . . .
> But for Christ the crucified
> Not a place that He could enter.

I once read that Harriet Beecher Stowe wrote *Uncle Tom's Cabin* in odd moments between cooking meals and looking after her six children. Her biographer commented: "Had she waited until she had more time, that bestseller would probably never have been written."

Some of you will, I hope, remember the name

of Professor Gordon Hamilton Fairley, the cancer expert who was killed by a bomb a few years ago. His widow Daphne declared afterwards that she felt no trace of bitterness. She went on: "We, as a family . . . pray that we will learn something invaluable from our loss. If you want to do something – do it today. Say sorry – show somebody you love them now. If you've had a row, make it up. Don't waste time. We never did."

Suppose that each of us were born with a little gadget on our shoulder which from our first moment showed the number of hours left to us. It would begin with a reading of, say, half a million. That would steadily decline. One day we would have only a quarter of a million hours left; then we would have only a hundred thousand; then just ten thousand; then just a thousand, then a hundred, then twenty-four, then three, two, one – zero! That would be rather unnerving, wouldn't it? But it would make us appreciate time more. As the hours were slowly but surely ticked off we would try to use every one to the utmost, wouldn't we?

The verse goes:

If time were something we could buy,
To hoard or throw away,
Would anybody term as high
The price we'd have to pay?
If time were something that could be
Either bought or sold,
It wouldn't take us long to see
The fading worth of gold.

These inspiring lines were published anonymously some years ago:

Take time to think — it is the source of power.

Take time to play — it is the secret of perpetual youth.

Take time to read — it is the fountain of wisdom.

Take time to pray — it is the greatest power on earth.

Take time to love and be loved — it is a God-given privilege.

Take time to laugh — it is the music of the soul.

Take time to give — it is too short a day to be selfish.

Take time to work — it is the price of success.

An old friend of mine calls himself "seventy years young". I asked him the secret of his happiness, and he smiled. "When I was young I used to worry a lot," he said. "One day somebody with whom I had shared my worries asked me, 'What were you worrying about ten years ago?' 'Don't be daft,' I replied. 'How can I remember that?' 'Well,' said my friend, 'ten years from now you won't remember what you were worrying about today!'"

I like the story of the fourteen year-old lad who started work on a farm as a shepherd's boy. He became a shepherd in his own right and served three generations of the same family. After sixty-five years of work on the same farm, his employer gently suggested that it might be a good time to retire, since he was now seventy-nine. But the shepherd was deeply offended by this. "Huh!" he retorted, "if I'd known the job was just temporary, I'd never have taken it!" You're as young as you feel!

There is a Golden Day in every week. Yesterday we can do nothing about, for it is past. Tomorrow is still to come. But today, the Golden Day, is ours to do with as we wish. *Live for the Golden Day*.

The well-known Gospel song goes:

> One day at a time, sweet Jesus . . .
> That's all I'm asking of You . . .
> Just give me the strength to do every day
>   what I have to do.

A Dutch clockmaker had just finished making two identical grandfather clocks. One of the clocks asked its maker how hard it would have to work and how many times it would have to tick during its life. The clockmaker replied that with 1,800 ticks per hour, the total number of ticks would be many millions. The clock thought about this, then worried about it for a long time and then died of anxiety, coming to a complete stop! The other clock decided not to ask too many questions and not to look too far ahead. Instead it would live one day at a time and just tick away quietly, facing the minutes and hours as they came. That clock lasted for hundreds of years, keeping perfect time!

Will Rogers, the famous star of silent films, was once asked this question: "If you had only twenty-four hours left to live, how would he spend them?" He replied, "One at a time." Jesus said, "do not worry about tomorrow, for tomorrow will worry about itself. Each day has enough trouble of its own" (Matthew 6:34). We should live a day at a time, in the present. That is the way to live life to the full.

50. Begin!

In the first verse of the Acts of the Apostles Luke writes, "In my former book, Theophilus, I wrote about all that Jesus began to do and to teach . . ." Jesus began His great mission and task, and He carried it through to completion on the Cross. How often we talk about doing some task or project without ever actually *beginning* it.

John Masefield, a former British Poet Laureate, wrote:

> Sitting still and wishing
> Makes no person great;
> The good Lord sends the fishing,
> But you must dig the bait.

What's keeping you from starting? *Begin now* to

pursue a goal
realise a dream
execute a plan
start a project
grab an opportunity
work at an idea
tackle a problem
make a decision.

Maybe there is a lesson for us in the classical story of Ulysses, who had to sail between Scylla (a sea monster) and Charybdis (a whirlpool). To go too close to either meant certain death. Ulysses did the only thing he could do – he steered as near the middle as he could. He risked losing everything, but he came through triumphantly. That is just what we must do in life – we must begin, we must take a risk. We may lose something in the process, but it will be worth it. We must always go forward! Begin today to

    uncover new opportunities!
    discover lovely solutions!
    overcome serious hindrances!
    unwrap the exciting surprises which God has in
      store for you!
    roll back the dark clouds until you see the glorious
      sunshine!

I once knew a couple who went through a very hard time indeed. Their only child died soon after his birth, and his mother became seriously ill afterwards. The father himself was shattered by his experiences in the Second World War, and returned home to find himself facing immense difficulties. Both he and his wife were nervous wrecks and they had barely enough to live on. The couple began to contemplate suicide. But it was at that point that a neighbour looked in on them and told them he had an old handcart they could use if they wanted to. He suggested they might try collecting and selling junk. The couple stared at him listlessly, but then a flame of hope flickered in their hearts. Doing something, even collecting junk, was better than doing nothing and wasting away. So they began a little junk business. Slowly but steadily it grew, and they won back their health. Eventually they even adopted two children. It is so important to *begin*, even if we cannot see where it will lead us.

We must begin, we must get going. Like many teenage boys, Peter was very slow to get going. He just wouldn't get up in the morning. Also, he often came in late at night. So Dad had a serious chat with him. "And remember," he said in conclusion, "it's the early bird that catches the worm."

Peter pretended to be puzzled. "But Dad, if the stupid worm hadn't been up so early, it would never have been caught by the bird!"

"Not at all, son," said Dad, rallying magnificently. "That worm was on its way home!"

Sir James Young Simpson pioneered the use of chloroform as an anaesthetic. He was criticised by ignorant medical men who said chloroform was harmful, by those who contended that it was immoral and by religious people who claimed that its use interfered with divine laws. But he fought on, and he won in the end. All the world owes a debt of gratitude to this man, who wore himself out in serving humanity. As he was dying he asked a friend at his bedside how old he was. "You're fifty-six," replied the friend. "Oh, well . . ." murmured Simpson. "I just wish I'd been busier . . . I wish I had begun sooner . . ."

The old verse goes:

Begin today and do what you can,
Being what you are.
Shine like the glow-worm if you cannot be a star,
Work like a pulley if you cannot be a crane,
Be a wheel-greaser if you cannot drive the train.
Use your brain, by beginning again.

Begin with God, for your life is far better with Him in it. In Bunyan's *Pilgrim's Progress* it says, "Christian slept till the break of day, then he awoke and sang . . . and began . . ." I love that sentence, and I try to live it every day.

"In the beginning was the Word . . ." (John 1:1). Jesus was there at the Beginning. He is the Great Initiator. He never misses an opportunity to reach out and take our requests and make them His own. He is always "on the ball". He is "the Beginning and the End" (Revelation 21:6).

51. Humility

What is true humility? We may think that the quiet old lady who always sits at the back of the church and never gets in anyone's way, who never does anything that people notice but just comes faithfully to church every Sunday, is an example of humility. Well, perhaps, but not necessarily. True humility is an inner attitude of the heart, a yielding of oneself.

Hudson Taylor once said that humility was "being small enough for God to use". The great evangelist D. L. Moody used to say, "You can be too big for God to use, but never too small." To "eat humble pie" is the only way to move upward and forward in Christ. Augustine said, "It was pride that turned angels into devils, and it is humility that turns men into angels."

John Bunyan wrote glowingly of this blessed virtue of humility:

> He that is down, needs no fall,
> He that is low, no pride;
> He that is humble, ever shall
> Have God to be his guide.

Here is a paraphrase of a Quaker song from about two hundred years ago:

It's a gift to be humble,
It's a gift to come down to where we ought to
 be.
When we see ourselves in a way that is right
We will live in a valley of love and delight . . .
When true humility is gained . . .
To live and to love we will not be ashamed.

If people parade their "humility" they show that they
in fact have none! A man once wrote a book entitled
Humility and How I Achieved It. The character
Uriah Heap in Dickens' *David Copperfield* must be
the most famous instance of false humility. "I am
well aware I am the humblest person going," he said.
There are many people who are not quite so blatant
as that, but they are quietly proud of their humility
– proud that they are not proud!

Having spent a time alone in the desert, Saint
Anthony came to the conclusion that there could be
no holier saint than he. Later, in the back streets
of a great city, he met an old cobbler named Conrad.
Anthony asked him, a little haughtily, what he had
ever done to please the Lord. "Me?" Conrad replied.
"Me? I have done nothing but mend sandals. But,"
he said, raising his head, "I have mended each pair
as though they belonged to my Lord and Saviour."
That simple cobbler taught Anthony a lesson he
never forgot.

If we think we are humble, then we are not! Three
monks of different orders were talking together one
day. One of them, a Dominican, said, "Our order
is the best, because we are the intellectuals of the
Church." A second, who was a Jesuit, said, "Oh no,

ours is the greatest order, because it is the most disciplined." The third, who was a Franciscan, piped up: "We are the most noble of orders because we are the humblest!"

A schoolboy who had been cheeky to a teacher was given a severe dressing down by the Headmaster and was warned that if he erred again he would be in for some tough punishment. "You ought to be more modest and humble, boy," the Head told him. The boy promised to obey. The following week the boy was again brought before the Head for bad behaviour. "You promised me you would be more modest and humble!" he said. The boy sheepishly replied, "I tried for a week, sir, but no-one noticed!" Here is a true old saying: "Modesty does nothing to be noticed, but cannot in the end be missed."

History contains many examples of humility but, of course, Jesus Himself is the supreme example. He gave up the glory of heaven to come to earth for our sakes. Paul wrote: "Christ Jesus . . . being in very nature God, did not consider equality with God something to be grasped, but made himself nothing, taking the very nature of a servant, being made in human likeness. And being found in appearance as a man, he humbled himself and became obedient to death – even death on a cross! Therefore God exalted him to the highest place . . ." (Philippians 2:5-9).

Humility is mentioned many times in Scripture. It exhorts us to "put on . . . humbleness of mind" (Colossians 3:12), to "walk humbly" (Micah 6:8), to be "clothed with humility" (1 Peter 5:5). God has said, "This is the one I esteem: he who is humble and contrite in spirit, and trembles at my word" (Isaiah 66:2). Jesus said, "Come to me . . . learn from me, for I am gentle and humble in heart" (Matthew 11:28-29).

The Bible places great emphasis on humility as a vital condition for gaining success in life: "Clothe yourselves with humility towards one another, because 'God opposes the proud but gives grace to the humble.' Humble yourselves, therefore, under God's mighty hand, that he may lift you up in due time" (1 Peter 5:5-6). God has promised special success, exaltation, blessing, victory and prosperity to the humble. As Jesus said, "he who humbles himself will be exalted" (Luke 14:11).

In fact God has said that humility is the key to revival: "if my people, who are called by my name, will humble themselves and pray and seek my face and turn from their wicked ways, then will I hear from heaven and will forgive their sin and will heal their land" (2 Chronicles 7:14). In 1951-52 a powerful revival swept through the Hebrides Islands in Scotland. It was the last great revival to touch Britain. Even today its effects can be felt – for example, the churches are still crowded on Sundays. I went to the islands recently and sought to discover its secret. I think it was summed up in these words spoken by Duncan Campbell, the great man of God who was used so mightily by the Lord during the revival: "The key to God's supernatural visitation of these Islands was a spirit of exceeding deep humility, holiness,

210

love and persistency in intercession." If we want to see revival in our land, we must first humble ourselves before God.

52. Famous but Humble

In order to serve God we need drive and positiveness, but we also need humility. In fact all of the most successful Christian leaders I have rubbed shoulders with have been modest and humble people. Also, quite a number of the famous figures of the past have been unassuming folk, seemingly unaffected by their fame.

George Washington was once out riding with some friends in the country. One of their horses happened to kick a few stones from the top of a wall it had leaped over.

"We'd better put those stones back," said Washington.

"Oh, we can leave that to the farmer," said one of his companions.

But when the ride was over Washington went back to the wall and began to carefully replace the stones.

"But General," protested one of his friends, "you are too big a man to do that!"

"On the contrary," replied Washington. "I am just the right size."

Samuel Chadwick once humbly volunteered to clean someone's boots. As he was on his knees doing this menial task he felt Jesus' presence. There and then he vowed that in future, whatever he did he would do for the Lord. He went on to become one of the greatest Christian teachers of his age!

Once one of the Dukes of Norfolk happened to be at the railway station near his home, Arundel Castle, when a little Irish girl stepped off the train with a very heavy bag. She had come to join the Duke's household staff as a maidservant. Timidly she asked a porter if he would carry her bag to the castle, which was about a mile away. She offered him a shilling, which was all the money she had, but the porter contemptuously refused. Then the Duke stepped forward, in somewhat shabby dress as usual. He picked up her bag and walked the mile with her, chatting to her as they went. At the castle gate he took the shilling she offered him and waved goodbye to her. It was only the next day, when she met her employer, that the girl knew that it had been the Duke of Norfolk himself who had carried her bag from the station for a shilling! The truly great man does not think of his place or prestige. It is only little people who are concerned with their status.

King Edward VII had been having lunch with his friend, David Sassoon, at his home in Hove in Sussex. As he left Sassoon's house a schoolboy who had been waiting outside asked him the time. The King consulted his watch. "Half past three," he said.

"Half past three?" exclaimed the boy. "Crumbs, it's later than I thought. They say the blooming old King's inside this house – I've been hanging around since one o'clock to see him! But I ain't waiting no longer – he ain't worth it!"

King Edward had turned sixty but had never quite

grown up. Instead of being annoyed he was tickled pink by the loyal but weary laddie. "You're right," he declared warmly, "absolutely right, sonny. He just ain't worth it. Anyhow, there's no need for you to wait any longer. I'm the blooming old King, and here's something to remember me by."

A few silver coins changed hands, and the astonished boy went off with his head in a happy whirl.

Isobel Baillie's beautiful voice made her a household name in her time. But although she was famous she was also remarkably modest. In her autobiography the actress Beryl Reid recalls that when she was a child she used to visit Isobel's home to play with her daughter. Beryl grew up and didn't see Isobel for years, but there came a time when they happened to be on the same programme at the Albert Hall. Beryl was delighted to see Isobel again. The great singer told her that she had always followed her career with great interest and had gone to see everything she had done on stage. "But why didn't you come and see me?" asked Beryl. "Oh," replied Isobel, "I didn't think you would remember me."

I like this story which Sinclair Lewis, the famous American novelist, once told against himself. One day during a crossing of the Atlantic on a liner he and a friend were pacing the deck. They passed a woman who was sitting in a deckchair reading. Lewis was delighted to see that she was reading a book which he had written. Pulling his friend aside, he whispered to him, "Look, she's reading one of my books! That's fame! There is an obviously intellectual woman absorbed in what I have written!"

But the next moment the woman shut the book with a snap and contemptuously tossed it overboard. Lewis felt very humbled!

One of the things I love best about children is that they can be so natural and so lacking in the pride which adults display. Princess Margrethe, who is today the popular and lovely Queen of Denmark, was as a schoolgirl once asked by a new girl in her class, "What's your father?" She replied, "He's a king. What's yours?" We adults need to emulate the unselfconscious humility and modesty of children.

A certain well-known preacher was recently conducting some crusades in Queensland in Australia. He was invited to meet with and speak to a gathering of fourteen young ministers and evangelists in a remote part of the Outback. He agreed, and flew 600 miles and drove 250 miles on some very rough roads to meet these Christian workers. He was used to speaking to crowds of hundreds and thousands, but he didn't mind that there were only going to be fourteen people listening to him. He felt that God wanted him to go and speak to them, so off he went. He knew that even one person is of inestimable value to Jesus. I suggest that the minister who is too big to speak to just a handful of folk is too big!

An amusing story is told of a church service at which the preacher was to be a visiting dean. The vicar rose and proceeded to give the dean a long and elaborate introduction, listing his many splendid achievements. At last the vicar stopped, and the dean, who had been rather embarrassed by all this praise, was greatly relieved. On his way to the pulpit the dean turned to the vicar and said, "Thank you. After an introduction like that I can hardly wait to hear what I've got to say!"

I heard a lovely story recently. When the House of Commons was being constructed a painter requested permission to paint one of the large frescoes. He added that if that request could not be granted, he would like permission to paint one of the small frescoes. Then he said that if that request could not be granted either he would like permission to mix the paint for the man who did the painting. He was so eager to be involved in the work that he was willing to do even the most humble part of it. That should be our attitude. If someone else is asked to do the "big" jobs which get all the attention, so be it. We should be content to be able to serve God in some way, no matter how small. Let us pray, "Lord, keep us humble and modest!"

53. "It's Been Sent to Try Us!"

That's what my wonderful Grandmother often used to say. I'm not sure that she was always right to say that — I think Satan rather than God was the source of many of the severe hardships which she suffered. But I'm certain that she was right to adopt an attitude of fortitude in the face of suffering.

I like this old Scottish proverb: "Don't give up when the clouds surround you — it might be a sign that you're climbing higher!" Here's another old saying which is worth remembering: "When you come to the end of your tether, remember that God is holding the other end."

Paul Brickchill's book *Reach for the Sky* tells the inspiring story of the life of Group Captain Douglas Bader. He had lost both his legs in a plane crash and was hovering between life and death in a hospital bed. He happened to hear someone in the corridor outside his room telling someone else to be quiet. "There's a boy dying in there," the person said. The shock of those words awoke in him a fierce determination to live. From that moment he fought his way back to life. He went on fighting, and eventually became a distinguished RAF hero in the Battle of Britain. His story is a lesson to us all on the power of sheer determination.

In difficult times determination is all-important:

> When everything is wrong as wrong,
> And you yourself are wrong side out;
> When folk or things just make you want
> To weep alone, or loudly shout;
> For goodness sake count up to ten,
> Then grit your teeth and start again.

One must press through and turn disasters and difficulties into triumphs. Gideon did just that. In the power of the Spirit of God he took on a fierce, well-armed and numerous enemy with only three hundred men and a few lamps and empty jars – and he overcame them and won the day!

One must press on and never quit. The old verse goes:

> Something comes and hits you hard,
> Knocks you flat as flat;
> Makes you sorry for yourself –
> Nasty business, that.
>
> Will you keep on lying there,
> Crushed by grief or pain?
> Guess you'll stir yourself somehow
> And get up again!

A well-known journalist wrote some years ago about an incident in his childhood:

When I was a schoolboy aged about nine, my home was about two miles from school. Cycling there on a bright sunny morning was easy as pie, because the road was downhill almost all the way. Coming home, however, was another story — pedalling uphill was a tiring job.

One winter's day I cycled home after darkness had fallen. Street lamps were very few and far between. I pedalled on and on till suddenly I stopped short. A street lamp at a corner lit up my house . . . I had arrived sooner than expected, less tired than before. And then, very puzzled, I realised what had happened. I'd been pedalling into the darkness, seeing only a few square yards of what looked like a flat road picked out by the short, weak beam of my cycle lamp.

Even at the early age of nine I realised that if you don't keep looking up your hill, climbing it is easier.

This story shows that the way in which we look at our troubles and trials is of great importance. Only the other day I was looking for a book in the library and quite by chance picked up a copy of *Love at Paddington* by William Pett Ridge, who died over forty years ago. Thumbing through it, I found a simple bit of philosophy. The writer recommended that if we want to look at trouble we should use opera glasses, and use them the wrong way round. Then it will look very small indeed!

God has promised to help us in our "downs", in our times of trouble: "The Lord is a refuge for the oppressed, a stronghold in times of trouble" (Psalm 9:9). How good it is to be able to trust a higher power so completely with one's life!

David Livingstone, the famous explorer and

missionary, was once stuck on the bank of a river for days because his native followers were afraid to cross over, since they were in the territory of a hostile tribe. Eventually Livingstone decided that the crossing would have to be made, and that the only time to do it was night-time. In preparing himself for this, he opened his Bible and read to himself the promise which Jesus had made to His disciples: "Lo, I am with you alway" (Matthew 28:20). Then he told his followers that they were going to cross the river at once. "But what about the enemy?" they cried. "We will all be killed!" "Jesus will be with us," he replied. "He has promised to be with us always, and He never breaks His word." The crossing was duly made, and there was not a single casualty.

Recently someone showed me the words and music of a fine new hymn entitled "By the Rutted Roads We Follow". It is a hymn for springtime and speaks about ploughing and planting and about the patience and care that are needed before a harvest can be reaped. In a sense it is a parable about the secret of living. But what intrigued me most was the name of the author – John Arlott. Could this be the John Arlott who used to be a radio cricket commentator? It is indeed the same man. His life has brought him many bitter experiences. For four years he worked in a mental hospital. For eleven years, including those of the last war, he was a policeman in Southampton, and there he witnessed the tragedy and devastation of those terrible times. His eldest son was killed in a car crash at the tender age of twenty. Now, in this hymn, John Arlott shares with us the faith that has carried him through all this. It inspires us, in the face of suffering and tragedy, to make a new beginning on life's road.

54. Turning Tragedy into Triumph

I always like to read of people who have turned stumbling-blocks into stepping-stones, who have changed some awkward situation into something useful. William the Conqueror was one of those people. When he set foot on English soil at Pevensey in 1066 he stumbled and fell full-length. The Norman soldiers at once took this to be a bad omen. Not so Duke William of Normandy. He immediately got to his feet, grasping in each hand some of the earth on which he had fallen. "Look!" he cried, holding up the handfuls of soil. "This is a sign that God has delivered this land into my hands!" With this adroit manipulation of a mishap William rallied his army and so won the Battle of Hastings.

For three weeks the musician Arthur Sullivan had spent every night at the bedside of his only brother, whom he loved dearly. On the last night, when his brother was evidently sinking, Arthur was tired and distressed, unable to watch and unable to leave the room before the end came. Pacing about, he picked up a book and turned its pages idly. He found himself reading some verses written by Adelaide Ann Proctor. Suddenly a few of her lines gave him the idea for a song. There and then on a piece of paper he composed the song which was to be known as "The Lost Chord". It is remarkable that out of Sullivan's personal sorrow and heartbreak should come a much-loved song that would be sung around the world and would touch the hearts of millions. In a similar way God can bring out of the suffering, tragedy and darkness in our lives treasures of light, faith, victory and success.

If you visit Warwick Castle you may be fortunate enough to be taken around it by a guide named Edward Miller. He has a wonderful gift for making the history of this beautiful place come alive. His style is precise, interesting, vivid and humorous. He knows every corner of the castle and can answer any and every question about it. What makes him all the more remarkable is that he is blind!

During the last war he suffered terrible injuries and, worse still, lost his sight. He had to spend a long time in hospital, and when he was finally able to leave it seemed that he had little prospect of being able to work. But then he was given the chance of becoming a guide at Warwick Castle. To learn all its history and to get to know its every detail would have been a challenge for any man. For Edward, who had never seen the castle, it must have been a daunting task, to say the least. But he rose to the challenge and learned all there was to learn about the castle. Today, if you follow him around the chapel, for example, he will point out to you beautiful things that might otherwise have escaped your notice – such as the wonderful light on the face of Jesus in an old painting, the magnificent colours of which have remained unfaded for seven hundred years; or perhaps an intricate carving, half hidden in the darkness. So, blind as he is, Edward is opening the eyes of others to the secrets of the castle. He has turned his personal tragedy into a triumph. His story has a lot to teach us. Have you learned its lesson? Do you wallow in your failures and tragedies, or are you someone who "perseveres under trial" (James 1:12)?

Some years ago I met a Scottish farmer named Tom Borthwick. He owned a large dairy farm and was a highly successful man. And yet he had started out with nothing. His father had been very poor and Tom had had a hard boyhood. So how did he achieve such wealth? He simply made a decision one day that he would become a rich farmer! "I started my herd," he told me, "buying them one at a time and buying nothing but kickers." "What's a kicker?" I asked. "A kicker is a cow which is good enough but is temperamental and difficult to milk. I used to buy them for next to nothing. I milked them all myself, night and morning." How often the way to success lies in turning difficulties into opportunities!

A young woman had become very ill. As a result she had failed all her exams and so had lost the chance of obtaining the interesting and affluent lifestyle which she had been hoping for. In despair she went to see her kindly old grandfather. When she arrived she was feeling very depressed and sorry for herself. "Why does everything go wrong for me?" she complained. "I don't know, my dear," replied her grandfather. "But there are some things I do know, and I'll tell you one of them now. You know, the wood for the best violins is taken from the windward side of the tree. And why? Because that's the side which suffers the most and so produces the finest wood. Think about that, my lass!" She did, and felt much better as a result! Trying times tend to either make people or break them. Often they bring out the best in them.

I was once playing snakes and ladders with a little boy. He was ill at the time and was feeling a bit down. He was finding the game a bit frustrating too, since he seemed to be getting more snakes than ladders. At last he burst out, "Wouldn't it be more fun if we went up the snakes and as well as the ladders?" I'm sure many of us have had thoughts like that about life – we've wished that it were all ups and no downs. But if life were like that, there would be no challenges in it. We would never have the opportunity to triumph over adversity.

55. The Noble People of the World

I was on a month-long church-planting mission in France. I had just had a successful but exhausting week, so I was having a day off. A young French couple had offered to show me around the area, which was close to the First World War battlefields. They took me to see Vimy Ridge, Arras and the villages and memorials of the Somme. Then as dusk was falling we came to a British graveyard, one of two hundred in the area for British personnel alone. I asked my French friends to stay at the gate, and for half an hour or so, in the twilight of that cold, November day, I walked amongst the ten thousand neatly laid-out graves. Most of the men had been just eighteen or nineteen years of age. Many of the stones bore beautiful scriptures. One said, "From Mum and Dad, to our only child." In one place two teenage brothers lay side by side. The stone marking the grave of a twenty-nine year-old man revealed that he had left four children behind.

Tears filled my eyes. I recalled Enoch Powell's words, "Will we ever see such Englishmen again?" A war poet had described them as "those men with splendid hearts". One million dead had been buried there in the pastureland of the Somme vale. It was a sombre place to be that evening: the sky was darkening and even the rooks in the dark branches of the trees seemed dressed for mourning and lamenting.

I prayed for a brave spirit to confront the enemy which I had to face in my own generation, and to fight valiantly as all these young men had done. In the gathering evening mist I took one last, long look at the white stones, standing row upon row upon row. From my pocket I drew a piece of paper bearing some words written by the poet Rupert Brooks:

> If I should die, think only this of me,
> That there's some corner of a foreign field
> That is forever England . . .

Shortly after my time in France I conducted the funeral of my great uncle, Percy Humphries. A veteran of the First World War, he died at the age of eighty-four. He was one of the few servicemen from Chippenham who came back from France. He flew in those flimsy old biplane fighters, when the average pilot's life expectancy at the front was just four days. What brave men they were!

I have met a number of truly gallant folk in my time. They have never hit the headlines or received any medals for their courage. They have been people of sterling character who have deeply influenced my life. Their composure and triumphant faith in the midst of life's severest tests have challenged and rebuked me and have given me fresh heart. These people have taught me to get my priorities right, and I am very grateful for that.

A few years ago in the Lebanon a bus was taking some girls home from school. Suddenly it went out of control as it started going down a steep hill. The driver panicked and leaped out. The bus careered down the hill. At the bottom of it there was a fifteen-foot-high wall, and the bus crashed straight into this. Twenty-three of the schoolgirls on the bus were killed outright, but one of them survived, although maimed and paralysed for life. She had to spend a long time in hospital. At first she felt very bitter and just wanted to die, believing that her life was ruined. In spiritual agony she called out to God to help her. Then she had a remarkable experience. Her soul was suddenly flooded with a wonderful peace. She felt a new inner power that changed her life completely. Eventually she was taken to England to be rehabilitated.

I had the privilege of meeting her when I once visited Stoke Mandeville Hospital. She exuded a radiant and triumphant faith. The memory of her will never be erased from my mind. "I know that Christ is real," she told me. "If I had to choose, I would rather be paralysed and experience this power of Christ in my life than have the use of my legs and not know this inward assurance and strength." When I asked her what she planned to do with her life now she replied, "I have dedicated my life to helping orphaned children in my own country."

People like that young lady are the noble people of the world. They have a bearing and dignity that demands respect. Their lives are a powerful and convincing sermon. In their presence one has to listen. To offer them advice is almost irreverent. They have learned the great lesson about how to face life.

The early Christians nearly gave way to despair when Stephen, one of their leaders, was stoned to death. Peter had been set free from prison by angels, so why had God allowed this to happen? But from this disaster emerged brave Christian men and women who were to turn their world upside down.

Job experienced great suffering, but he lived to see the wonderful purpose of God for his life unfold into a meaningful pattern. Everything fitted in perfectly. The darkness in his life gave way to light. He received beauty instead of ashes and the oil of gladness instead of mourning, and in later life he was more blessed than he had ever been before, including a miraculous healing.

The great lesson to be learned is that when we submit humbly to God, He begins to work in our circumstances. The trouble with most of us is that the moment anything strange or adverse happens to us we think of it as a calamity instead of believing that God is working things out for our eternal benefit. We need to take to heart these words which Cowper wrote:

God moves in a mysterious way
His wonders to perform;
He plants His footsteps in the sea,
And rides upon the storm.

Faith Unlimited

Ye fearful saints, fresh courage take!
The clouds ye so much dread
Are big with mercy, and shall break
In blessings on your head.

56. Go Over, Not Under

In chapter 14 of Matthew's Gospel we read that when Jesus walked on the water to the disciples in the boat, Peter said to Jesus, "Lord, if it's you, tell me to come to you on the water." Jesus replied, "Come." So Peter got out of the boat and walked out to where Jesus was. "But when he saw the wind, he was afraid and, beginning to sink, cried out, 'Lord, save me!' Immediately Jesus reached out his hand and caught him" (verses 28-31). Jesus didn't let him go under.

The same is true for us today. God wants all of His people to discover that by His grace they have the ability to *go over* rather than *go under* in the face of life's difficulties. Seafaring tradition has it that captains go down with their ships when they sink. But God doesn't want us to go down with the ship. We may face great problems in our lives, but God wants us to stay afloat, to be victorious.

Of course, the secret of "going over" in life is in our attitude to the trials, troubles and strains which we face. An old verse goes:

Did you tackle the trouble that came your way
With a resolute heart and cheerful,

Or hide your face from the light of day
With a craven heart and fearful?
Oh, a trouble's a ton or a trouble's an ounce,
A trouble is what you make it,
And it isn't the fact that you're hurt that counts,
But only — how did you take it?

An American little girl named Doris Hart was stricken by polio, which left her with a crippled leg. Her parents were advised that she should take up tennis as therapeutic exercise for it. Doris was determined to overcome her handicap, but in the end she did far more than that. She became a world-class player and won the Ladies' Singles trophy at Wimbledon in 1951. Moreover, she was outstandingly popular because of her fine sense of sportsmanship.

The Rev Arthur B. Jordan had a son at college. He was about to take his final examinations, and naturally his father asked him to get in touch as soon as the results were known. A few days later Mr Jordan received a telegram. It read: "Hymn 254, verse five, last two lines." Looking up the reference in *Hymns Ancient and Modern*, he read: "Sorrow vanquished, labour ended, Jordan passed." Victory was his!

We should take to heart these lines (which I have paraphrased somewhat):

If you can make a promise, and by that promise
    stand,
If you can take a beating, then shake the victor's
    hand,
If you can do a deed without looking for the glory,

Go Over, Not Under

If you can hold your tongue when you hear a
    gossip's story,
If you can make good better, and try to make bad
    good,
If you can keep your soul alive with the grace of
    God as food,
If you can carry on till life's craggy road should
    end,
Then remember your life was a lend,
To prove you can go over, not under . . .
So face the storm and go on right through,
Determined, for this is vital . . .

When the heart is near to breaking,
Rough your lonely road,
Hope extinguished, joy forgotten,
Grief and pain your load . . .
Plod on bravely through the darkness,
Groping all the way,
Till God brings you to the sunshine
Of a brighter day.

Stan hurt his knee when he was pushing his car. How
could he, or anyone, know that such a little injury
would totally change his life? Alas, it did. The leg
became worse and worse. Stan had to give up his
career as a sea-going engineer, and despite all that
the doctors could do, the infirmity continued to
spread. Today Stan is so completely paralysed that
he cannot even wiggle a toe of move a finger. He
lies in his bed day and night. His only occupation
is to watch television. The set has been mounted on
a special bracket near the ceiling, since he can't sit
up to watch it. And yet he has not allowed this

terrible misfortune to drive him to despair. "There are many cases worse off than me," he says. "After all, how many men of my age are still blessed with a wonderful mother to look after them?" In his spirit he is not going under – he is going over!

May the words of this poem be your testimony:

> Now, time and again I've felt
> This surely is the end.
> Life's finished, and in grief or shame
> I must go round the bend.
> A broken heart, a loss, a pain . . .
> No sun for me will shine again.
>
> Yet, strange to say, somehow, somehow,
> I've plodded on and on,
> And found, quite unexpectedly,
> That fears or griefs have gone,
> For dark and lonely paths have brought
> My feet to sunny ways unsought!

In the beautiful, leafy cemetery at Avebury in my beloved home county of Wiltshire I came across a gravestone bearing these moving words:

> Here lie the remains of S. W. Eilliton, who during the Boer War suffered an injury causing complete and utter immobility, but who somehow ran and kept ahead of the many stresses and strains of his hectic life.

He went over!

David prayed, "Leave me not, neither forsake me, O God of my salvation" (Psalm 27:9). Jesus will always hear a prayer like that. It is certain that He won't leave us when we are in trouble. He came to Peter's aid when he was about to sink beneath the waves. He came to Lazarus' tomb and raised him from the dead. He came to the disciples in the upper room, passing through locked doors to get to them. He came, and still comes, to multitudes of diseased and incurable folk – with mighty power to heal them! For He loves to see people go over and not go under!

57. Stick At It!

A grandmother was talking to her six year-old grandson. He told her that he had been running that afternoon in his school's Sports Day. She knew he wasn't very athletic, so she didn't ask him how he had done in case he was feeling ashamed about it. But in fact he wasn't upset at all, and proudly told her, "I was the only one to come in last!" That boy had the right attitude – a spirit of optimism and persistence!

It's so important to persist and stick at things. I like this poem, called *The Man Who Sticks*:

The man who sticks has the sense to see
He can make himself what he wants to be;
If he'll get off his coat and pitch right in –
Why, the man who sticks can't help but win!

Here is another poem which speaks about persistence:

They say that you just can't accomplish this thing,
  no matter how often you try it.
You've blundered and failed, but you know in
  your bones,
you've grit and you mean to apply it.

If tempted to give up the fight one dark day,
it's certain you'll very soon rue it.
You'd better keep on keeping on . . . keeping on
until with a grin you just do it!

The philanthropist Samuel Warren once remarked, "There are two kinds of persons in the world – those who think first of difficulties, and those who think first of the importance of accomplishment in spite of difficulties." This famous verse says the same thing:

"It can't be done," they said,
"And you may as well admit it."
So he tackled the thing that couldn't be done –
And he did it.

David Shepherd, the famous wildlife artist, once gave a demonstration of his painting technique on television. As he completed his picture he said, "Well, that's it, I think. Not that I'm really satisfied with it. I'm never satisfied. When you're satisfied you make no progress." That's true not only of painting but also of the whole of life.

One of the most notable of the historical characters who triumphed over difficulties was the famous Greek orator Demosthenes, who lived in the fourth century before Christ. As a young man he wanted to be a politician, but he had a dreadful stammer, a weak voice and diseased lungs. However, he was determined to succeed. He cured his stammer by talking with pebbles in his mouth. He gave his voice greater strength by going to the seashore every day and shouting at the waves. His determination swept away all obstacles and so he became one of the greatest orators of all time. Even Winston Churchill copied him in some ways.

We must aim high and persist until we achieve our goals. As the poet Robert Browning said,

> Ah, but a man's reach should exceed his grasp,
> Or what's a heaven for?

Although it is some years since I read Bunyan's *Pilgrim's Progress* in its entirety, I often turn to it and reread passages which have helped me in the past. One passage which I read when I am feeling a bit discouraged is one of the incidents in Interpreter's house. Christian is shown a fire burning in the grate. A man is constantly throwing water on it, but the fire continues to burn. The mystery is explained when Christian is taken to the next room where, through a hole behind the fireplace, another man is pouring oil, so keeping the fire burning. There are circumstances which "damp" our spirits and there are people who are "wet blankets". Sometimes people "pour cold water" on our ideas and suggestions. But there is an antidote to all this. If our determination is strong enough, it will be a fire which will withstand any amount of discouragement.

The late Dr William Barclay told the story of a trainee London taxi driver who had to study the maps of the city until he knew them by heart. In his examination he was asked the shortest route between two certain points in the city. Because of the answer he gave he failed the test. The route he had in mind would have been very short but would have meant taking his taxi down a long flight of steps and

through a passage wide enough only for pedestrians!
Short cuts are not always what they seem. We should
always keep in mind that most of the things in life
which are really worth having come to us only
through patience and effort. Let's not be deluded by
life's short cuts. It's persistence that wins in the end:

> One word won't tell folk who you are –
> You've got to keep on talking;
> One step won't take you very far –
> You've got to keep on walking;
> One inch won't make you very tall –
> You've got to keep on growing;
> One trip to church won't tell you all –
> You've got to keep on going.

As Paul advised – Praying always . . . in the spirit,
being watchful . . . to this end *with all perseverance*
(Ephesians 6:18).

58. It's a Wonderful Life!

The children crowded around it. "Wow! Look at that!" said one. "It's moving!" said another. "Is is a real one?" said a third. The youngsters were gazing in wonder at something. As I hurried by on my jog through the park I wondered what it was that had so caught their attention. I didn't stop to find out, but by their words, by the glint I had seen in their eyes, I knew that it must be something that was wonderful to such young, eager, fresh minds. Perhaps it was a baby sparrow, or a hedgehog, a toad, a mouse — who knows? Later I thought about how marvellous children's sense of wonder is. Our sophisticated adult world has lost it. Children can teach us adults so much about this wonderful life!

I was having a conversation with a neighbour one afternoon when her little girl came in to the room. "Mummy, Mummy!" cried the girl. "I've seen a lovely little bird in the garden!"

"This is Mr Banks," said her mother in icy tones. "Ask him how he is."

I saw the child's joy and excitement fade away before my eyes. "Good afternoon, Mr Banks . . . How are you?" she said in a voice as flat as a pancake. What could I say? I wanted to scream at her mother and gather the girl up in my arms and go out into the garden and share her little world of wonder. Of course, out of courtesy to her mother I just said, "Very well, thank you." Let us all take care not to crush the glorious, pioneering spirit of a child for the sake of empty politeness.

Mrs Jenny Wilson, of Edinburgh, has two daughters – Susan, who is eight, and Moira, who is five. Usually the sisters are the best of friends, but on one occasion they had an argument. It seemed to end in Susan's favour when she told her little sister severely, "Remember, I'm three years older than you!" There was silence for a moment. Then Moira retorted, "Well, *you* remember that I'm three years newer than you!" There was more in her words than she realised. It's so important to be "new", to have a fresh, childlike, open-eyed approach to life.

Many stories are told about Anna Pavlova, the celebrated Russian ballerina. One night, in Edinburgh, she danced her most famous role, the Dying Swan. There was a momentary silence before the rapturous applause broke out. In that silence a refined voice in the audience proclaimed loudly, "She's awfully like Mrs Wishart!" The woman had totally missed the brilliance of the great star's performance – she had been blind to the light, the colour, the movement, deaf to the music. All she could see was Pavlova's resemblance to one of her neighbours!

A story is told of an old cleaner who used to scrub the floor of an art gallery in the days when knees, buckets and scrubbing brushes were the main tools of the cleaner's trade. "What a lot of lovely paintings you have here," a visitor once said to her, gazing at the walls. "Yes, I suppose so – if you have the time to look up – which I don't," came the bleak retort. She was surrounded by beauty all the time, but she never bothered to appreciate it.

We are all a little like the girl in the story about the house with the golden windows. She used to gaze in wonder at the house across the valley because its windows shone like gold in the evening sunlight. She did not realise that to the people on the other side of the valley the windows of her own house looked just as golden. Let's look for the beauty which is close at hand!

Wilfred Shepherd was a Methodist minister whose church was almost in the shadow of Carlisle Cathedral. Over the years he spent many contented hours wandering around that historic building. He used to say, "He who has seen a cathedral a hundred times has undoubtedly seen something, whereas he who has seen a hundred cathedrals has seen nothing at all." He knew how to appreciate the beauty which was right on his doorstep. I think we sometimes miss much of the wonder which lies in the things and places which are familiar to us. Let's look – and look again – at our surroundings. We will probably see something we have never noticed before!

"Wonder" and "wonderful" are truly biblical words – they appear many times in Scripture. Mark writes, "As soon as all the people saw Jesus, they were overwhelmed with wonder and ran to greet him" (Mark 9:15). Luke writes, "they were filled with wonder and amazement at what had happened" (Acts 3:10). The Psalmist tells God, "Your statutes are wonderful" (Psalm 119:129). Habakkuk the prophet urged God's people to "observe, be astonished, wonder . . ." (Habakkuk 1:5). Joel saw "the earth and sky full of wonders" (Joel 2:30, NASB).

Do not miss the wonders which are around you. What is life worth when the beauty, love, appreciation, awe and wonder are gone? Wonder is one of life's greatest joys and excitements. Without it we slump into drudgery, boredom and scepticism. God is a God of wonder, marvel and omnipotence. Let us keep an attitude of wonder towards Him and towards His works and creation.

59. Thank God for Children

The most touching moments in my life are when I see a child healed from a disease. I often receive letters from parents whose children have been healed during my crusades. "Her incurable deafness is gone," writes one mother; "The skin disease that covered every inch of his body has vanished," writes another. One grandmother from Norfolk writes, "Our three year-old grandson was dying of leukaemia six months ago. We thought we wouldn't have him with us for very much longer. Then you and your colleagues prayed for him . . . his blood count doubled in a few days . . . Today he is a sturdy, ruddy-faced, fit and healthy lad . . . We thank God!"

I remember the time when a big, tall, tough-looking man brought his daughter to one of my meetings in Leigh in Lancashire. He had hardly ever been to church in his life, but he had heard about the miracles of healing that were happening, so he had brought his little girl in her wheelchair to see if anything could be done for her. God did a miracle that night. The child got up out of the wheelchair and walked up the aisle. The congregation applauded thunderously. Her father was overwhelmed, and, tough as he was, wept openly with happiness. I was so moved that I wept with him.

Children are so important and so precious. God saved the infant Moses from death and raised him up as a great leader of His chosen people, who were in the future to occupy the very centre stage of history. Time and again in the Bible God points to children as models of spiritual simplicity and goodness. Isaiah wrote of the coming Kingdom of God, "a little child will lead them" (Isaiah 11:6).

I am always moved by the true story of Queen Victoria and the Mudlark. The Mudlarks were poverty-stricken children from the East End of London who scratched out a living by beach-combing on the mudbanks of the Thames — hence their nickname. One night one of these youngsters got into Windsor Castle by stealth. He was quickly caught by the guards, but he got to meet the Queen. Since her husband's death ten years before she had been a virtual recluse and had hardly been seen in public at all. However, she was so moved by the boy's account of the abject poverty in which he and his kind had to live that she vowed to return to her needy subjects. From that time on she became greatly involved with philanthropic works, visiting the impoverished East End of the capital, helping the poor and touring the country to meet her people. This great change for the better was brought about through a simple child!

At the Battle of Waterloo the forces under the command of the Duke of Wellington, having withstood Napoleon's onslaught for many hours, were reaching breaking point. The day was saved when the mighty Prussian army, led by Marshal Blucher, arrived and turned the tide of the battle. They got there late in the day, but they might have been too late had a Belgian child not led them along a short cut to the scene of the battle.

It is the simplicity and guilelessness of a child which is so appealing. I like the story of the three year-old who had been taught by his mother to be careful with other people's property. One day when he was at his grandmother's he spilled some orange juice on the lawn. He dashed into the kitchen and ran out again with a cloth. "Whatever is the matter, Tommy?" his mother asked him. "Granny won't want her grass spoiled!" he answered.

Another little boy was at a birthday party and was asked by the hostess if he would like some more jelly. "Yes please," he answered. "Mum said I wasn't to ask for a second helping, but she didn't know how small the first helpings were going to be!"

A little girl was washing her pet kitten. "I don't think Mother Cat would like you to use quite so much water as that," said the girl's mother. "Cats don't like water, you know." The girl frowned. "But what else can I do, Mummy?" she asked. "I can't lick the kitten clean!"

A schoolteacher admonished a boy for handing in an essay which was exactly the same as the one his brother had written. "How do you explain this?" asked the teacher. "Well, sir, we have the same mother!" was the prompt reply.

Jesus placed a very high value on children and prized their innocence. "It would be better for [someone] to be thrown into the sea with a millstone tied round his neck than for him to cause one of these little ones to sin" (Luke 17:2). He welcomed them with open arms, saying, "Let the little children come to me, and do not hinder them, for the kingdom of heaven belongs to such as these" (Matthew 19:14). He told the adults of his day that they had to be childlike to be saved, that they had to be innocent, simple, sincere, believing and trusting in their approach: "unless you change and become like little children, you will never enter the kingdom of heaven" (Matthew 18:3).

I love the candour of a child — I love those big, wide, open eyes that look up at you, asking for a sweet or a gift or your attention.

> He who gives a child a treat
> Makes joy-bells ring in heaven's street.

May we truly love children, giving them treats, outings, kindness and our Christian heritage. May we teach them the wonders of the Bible and pray for them. Let us win them for Jesus and guard them and watch over them. They long for parental guidance, care and love.

A little girl often used to ask, "What is that old, old building, Mummy?" when she and her mother walked past the local church. Her mother would reply, "That's the house where Jesus lives." However, since she never, ever saw anyone in the windows and the place looked so old, she asked one day, "Is that the house where Jesus used to live?" Many family homes are places where Jesus used to live. Is that true of your household? Or do you still welcome Him in your home, teaching your children about

Him from the Bible? Only if we are doing this can our children have a reliable moral and spiritual background which will sustain them in later life. May we learn from our children, and may we give them the teaching, love and security which they long for.

60. Stable or Unstable?

How often one hears someone say, "He's a nice enough chap, but you can't rely on him!" So many people today seem to be unreliable and unstable. It's a disease of our time.

I once heard the story of a man who wanted to get to a certain village in Scotland called Mathons. Driving along, he came to a crossroads and saw a signpost which said it was four miles to Mathons one way and seven to Croxley the other way. Taking the Mathons road, he drove for four miles, but no village came in sight. Seeing a man working in the front garden of a cottage, he stopped. "Excuse me – am I on the road to Mathons?" he asked the man.

"Depends on which direction ye go," he replied. "If ye keep going the way you're headed now ye'll come to Croxley in about three miles. But if ye turn around and go back t'other way, ye'll get to Mathons in about eight miles."

"But the signpost at the crossroads said it was four miles to Mathons this way!"

"Maybe so," grinned the man, "but ye mustn't take any notice o' that thing – he twirls with the wind, he does!"

Many folk today are like that signpost – they

"twirl" with the slightest wind of changing moral standards. *How we need people today who are bastions of principle and truth and morality!*

In these days of moral compromise and weakness, people think that firm principles are to be found only in the realms of fantasy. A young man went into his local library and asked if they had a copy of a book entitled *Harmony in Marriage*. The librarian he spoke to thought for a moment and then asked doubtfully, "Is that fiction?"

People today are unstable and unreliable, but God is always sure and trustworthy: "I the Lord do not change" (Malachi 3:6); "The Lord is my rock, my fortress and my deliverer" (Psalm 18:2); "Jesus Christ is the same yesterday and today and for ever" (Hebrews 13:8).

Many people still remember how frightening it was in the early days of the Second World War, when the whole nation lived in dread of air raids. They were sad days, too, for countless children had to be evacuated from the towns and cities into the country. There they had to live amongst strangers, cut off from their homes and parents. One little boy found comfort in his bedtime prayers, in which he would ask God to take care of his loved ones. One night, after naming all those he wanted to be kept from danger, he paused for a moment. Then he burst out, "Oh, God, please look after Yourself, because if anything happens to You we're all sunk!"

Well, we can always be sure that nothing will happen to God – He will always be there on the scene. He will not leave us, He will never let us down. He is completely and utterly stable. He has enterd into a covenant with His people, and He will not break it: "He remembers his covenant for ever, the word he commanded, for a thousand generations" (Psalm 105:8). Remember His Word, His love, His peace, His grace. Be established, unmoveable, always anchored firmly in the Word of God — be stable!

61. The Little Things in Life

As I sit here writing there is a bunch of snowdrops in a little vase on my desk. They were picked by my wife in some nearby pretty woodlands here in beautiful Wiltshire. I am told that these flowers were first brought to this country by soldiers returning from the Crimean War. These delicate little plants were the only tender thing which the soldiers had to soften the harshness of their lives during the campaign.

There is another lovely story associated with snowdrops. It's said that when she was turned out of the Garden of Eden Eve wept bitterly for the flowers which she would not see any more. It was winter. Snow covered the barren ground and all was desolate. Then an angel took pity on her and caught a snowflake in his hand. He breathed on it and it fell to earth as a snowdrop. "This is an earnest, Eve, to thee," said the angel, "that sun and summer shall soon be here!"

Little things like snowdrops can be so full of joy and meaning for us. I think I enjoy the little things in life all the more because in my ministry I am concerned with the big issues of life – with people's salvation and healing, with their problems, their sicknesses, their divided homes, their pain-wracked minds and bodies. After a lengthly campaign I long to come home to Wiltshire and appreciate its beauty and quiet. This verse is very precious to me:

> Little songs to make me glad;
> Little comforts when I'm sad;
> Little chores at last well done;
> Little laughs and bits of fun;
> Little ills which happen not;
> Little nods that mean a lot;
> Little children to caress;
> Little deeds of tenderness . . .
> Such a wealth of little things
> To my spirit richness brings!

I heard recently about a washing line leading to an unforgettable evening. A Christian couple I know took an elderly lady for a drive in their car one evening. They hadn't gone far when she saw something which thrilled her. It was just a clothes line blowing in the wind! It was hooked to the wall of a picturesque country cottage at one end and to an apple tree at the other end. There was something appealing about the scene. The lady asked for the car to be stopped so that she could have a good look at it. A grey-haired lady peered at the car through a small window in the cottage and then came out to see what was going on. The two ladies got into a pleasant conversation, and it wasn't long before the grey-haired lady invited the other lady and the couple into her home. They all had a lovely chat together over tea and cake. They went on talking till after sunset, discussing their experiences and their mutual trust in God. So a mere washing line led to three people making new friends!

Canon Harry Twells was once invigilating at an examination. He sat watching the classroom full of boys scribbling away. He felt rather bored and weary, so he started jotting some words down. As the exam went on he carried on fiddling with his pen. By the end of the exam his scribblings had developed into a hymn. One of its verses went:

> Thy touch has still its ancient power,
> No word from thee can fruitless fall;
> Hear, in this solemn evening hour . . .
> And in thy mercy heal us all.

I have seen great numbers of people wonderfully converted and healed during the singing of that hymn! It's amazing that such a powerful song should have been written just because a minister's mind had wandered during an exam.

One day a little girl stood watching as her father and a shepherd who worked for him were talking. They were discussing what they should do with the dog which the shepherd was holding in his arms. Its leg had been broken. The men decided that it would have to be put down. However, the little girl took the dog away and for many weeks tenderly nursed it. Eventually it recovered the use of its leg and was able to run around again. That was Florence Nightingale's first medical experience, and she went on to pioneer the methods of modern nursing.

Let us thank God for the small things — for the snowdrops on my desk, for a washing line that brought people together, for a vicar's wandering

mind and pen, for a dog's broken leg that launched
a saint on a powerful mercy mission.

> I thank thee, Lord, that I can find
> In little things great joy . . .
> A little song, a little chat,
> A little girl and boy;
> So many little things there are
> To give our spirits wings.
> Lord, make me big enough, I pray,
> To love life's little things.

62. "Your Books are All About Nowt!"

The lovable stories written by James Herriot, the vet from North Yorkshire, are familiar to us all. They have been immensely popular all over the world, and are now selling even in Russia! However, once a blunt Yorkshire farmer told the writer, "Mr Herriot, your books are all about nowt!" He thought about this later, and decided that in a way the farmer had a point, because his stories are indeed all about life's little triumphs, disasters, struggles, battles and daily incidents. Yet the fact that they have sold so well surely shows that they have touched the hearts and imaginations of countless people. The "littleness" of the stories is the secret of their success. Most folk do not live "big" lives. They do not have the opportunity to bring about major events or make world-changing decisions. People's lives consist of their own and their families' daily trials, joys, mistakes, successes, losses and gains. For the most part people are concerned with their little daily victories, with the lessons they learn and with the small miracles that bring happiness and delight. These are the things that make up real life for most people.

"Your Books are All About Nowt!"

It's lots and lots of little knocks
That slowly get us down,
And rob each heart of joy and hope,
And give each face a frown.
It's little daily worries wear
Our tempers thin and bring despair.

But isn't it life's little joys
That bless and comfort one,
And give us strength each weary day
To keep on going on?
A little grit, a little smile,
Can make each little day worthwhile.

I once heard this delightful true story. A lorry laden with felled treetrunks one day arrived at a timber yard in Larbert in Scotland, having come many miles from Aberdeenshire. A crane was swung into position, and one by one the trunks were lifted off and taken away to be sawn up. Then a workman noticed something tucked away in the broken end of a beech trunk. The crane was stopped and the men gathered around. They were amazed to find a wren sitting on its nestful of eggs, watching them with beady eyes. Gently the trunk was taken to a quiet corner of the yard. The workmen left it untouched until the chicks had hatched and left the nest. Stories like that are very touching, aren't they? We all love life's little incidents.

A loving glance, a nod which says,
"Of course, I understand";
A shining hope, a sweet surprise,
The touch of someone's hand;

A misty dawn, a sparkling noon,
A sunset red and gold;
The little thrilling joys of youth,
Daydreaming when we're old . . .
These are the lovely, precious things
Which life to friendly people brings.

God, too, takes an interest in the simplest and tiniest aspects of our lives. Jesus said, "Are not five sparrows sold for two pennies? Yet not one of them is forgotten by God. Indeed, the very hairs on your head are all numbered" (Luke 12:6-7). Oh, the joys we miss because we do not appreciate the "nowts" of life. They have been given to us by our Creator to enrich our lives.

63. Sowing and Reaping

What memories I have of the reaping time in the Wiltshire of my youth! There was the smell of the corn, and the fine dust which got into your lungs and made you wheeze. There were the horsedrawn wagons taking away the bales of hay. There was the bright sunshine and the sweat on the farmers' faces. There was the harvesting machine, chugging away, dividing the corn from the hay.

Life is full of reaping and sowing. Scripture says, "The one who sows to please his sinful nature, from that nature will reap destruction" (Galatians 6:8). A visitor talking to an inmate in one of Her Majesty's prisons asked him what he was doing. "Are you sewing?" she enquired. "No, I'm reaping!" he replied with grim humour. He was suffering the results of his wrongdoing in the past. In life we reap whatever we sow.

This is a moral universe, and in it no one gets away with anything. For example, if you do nothing in your garden for a few months it will look dreadful! But if you plant and weed and sweat and watch and fertilise, you will get a very different result – a delightful garden, full of beautiful sights and smells.

Similarly, if you sin and try to bottle up your

feelings of guilt inside yourself, you will pay for it. Your guilt will reveal itself in your long face and your anxious behaviour. Macbeth's wife knew what it was to feel guilty: "What, will these hands ne'er be clean?" she asks in Shakespeare's play. "Here's the smell of blood still; all the perfumes of Arabia will not sweeten this little hand." She was reaping what she had sown.

There is no hiding from God. He has said, "Can anyone hide in secret places so that I cannot see him?" (Jeremiah 23:24) and "Your nakedness will be exposed and your shame uncovered" (Isaiah 47:3). God knows everything about us. Jesus said, "there is nothing hidden that will not be disclosed, and nothing concealed that will not be known or brought out into the open" (Luke 8:17). The Book of Hebrews says, "Nothing in all creation is hidden from God's sight. Everything is uncovered and laid bare before the eyes of him to whom we must give account" (Hebrews 4:13).

God neither slumbers nor sleeps; He is watching. No human eye saw David as he looked over the palace wall at Bathsheba and desired to have her, but God saw it, and He told Nathan the prophet to go to David and say, "You are the man!" (2 Samuel 12:7). Jonah stowed away in a boat, but God found him there. Elijah hibernated in a cave, but God located him. Zacchaeus hid in a tree, but Jesus told him to come down. God is big enough to be everywhere and small enough to be anywhere. If we are disobedient, we are found out. If we sin, our sin comes back to us. If we keep secrets, God knows them. As Paul says, the whole world is accountable to God, and every mouth is silenced in the face of His omniscience (Romans 3:19).

There is no way of escaping the consequences of our sins. In A. J. Cronin's novel *The Citadel* a young doctor fights for measures to improve the public health in a Welsh mining town. But he is defeated by local politicians, and in despair gives up his high moral standards and pursues wealth instead. But after his wife's tragic death he finds in her handbag some snapshots of himself during his crusading days, together with letters of gratitude from impoverished miners. He thinks bitterly about the man he might have been, and is consumed by remorse. "You thought you were getting away with it," he says to himself, "but, by God, you weren't!" He had discovered the biblical truth that we suffer the effects of our own sins.

God knows all about our transgressions and He judges us for the smallest of our sins, and yet *He is also looking for the slightest sign of repentance and change, for the smallest sowing of good seed in our lives*. Scripture tells us, "the one who sows to please the Spirit, from the Spirit will reap eternal life" (Galatians 6:8). Turn your sins over to God and in your heart sow good, pure, lovely thoughts. Then you will reap a good, healthy spiritual harvest.

PART III
SMITH
WIGGLESWORTH –
A MAN OF GOD

64. Turning Water into Petrol

One of the people who has influenced my life most of all has been the famous preacher Smith Wigglesworth. This great man of faith has inspired me for over thirty-five years. There are many remarkable stories about his life and ministry. In the next few chapters I shall be telling quite a number of them.

One night during the Second World War Wigglesworth was being driven by a minister named Harrison to Sutton-in-Ashfield in Nottinghamshire to preach at a meeting there. Suddenly the car's engine spluttered and the vehicle came to a halt. They were in the middle of the Sherwood Forest, seventeen miles away from their destination. "We shall never get to the meeting now," said Harrison. "The car's run out of petrol." (This sort of thing often happened during the war, since petrol was in very short supply, especially for private travel.)

Wigglesworth asked him, "Do you have any water?"

"Yes, I keep some for topping up the radiator."

"Put it in the petrol tank," boomed Wigglesworth.

Horrified by this idea, but not daring to disagree with the great man of faith, Harrison did as he was told. His hands shaking and trembling as he did it, he poured the water into the tank. He then revved the engine, and to his amazement the car started at the third try and got them to the meeting without any further problems. Harrison was utterly astonished by this, but he was sure that the engine must be a complete write-off after having all that water in it!

He happened to own a small factory, and so the next day asked one his workmen to make a special scoop which would fit into the neck of the petrol tank and, when withdrawn, would take a sample of the petrol out. The workman did this, and when Harrison took a sample he was amazed to find that it was pure petrol. There wasn't a trace of water!

What is all the more remarkable about this story is the fact that in those wartime days the petrol was dyed a different colour in each area of the country. This was to discourage people from wasting it. The police used to stop motorists and examine the colour of their petrol. If the colour wasn't that of the local area, it meant that the motorist was probably travelling further than he needed to. Now, the colour of the petrol in Harrison's car's tank was the Nottinghamshire colour. Not only had God, in response to Wigglesworth's faith, turned the water into petrol, but He had even made it the right colour!

On another occasion Wigglesworth was travelling by ship to preach in the States. He got talking to a fellow passenger. The man seemed rather depressed, and Wigglesworth asked him why. The man told him that he was taking hundreds of chickens of a special, fine breed to a customer in America. However, during the voyage the birds had become sick and had ceased to lay eggs. Obviously, the customer would not buy chickens which would not lay. This put the man in a desperate position, since the cost of transporting the chickens across the Atlantic had been considerable. He faced complete financial ruin.

However, Wigglesworth asked to be taken down into the hold. There he prayed over the sick birds while their owner stood and watched, fascinated, open-eyed and greatly puzzled. The preacher prayed, "O God, who has created every living thing, come now in power on these chickens, your creations, and set them free from barrenness and illness, so that they may lay eggs in abundance!"

The next day the owner was called down to the hold by the ship's stewards, who were complaining about the hundreds of eggs which the chickens had laid overnight. They were piled high in the cages! Every one was chock-a-block with big, beautiful, newly-laid eggs.

Wigglesworth was once preaching in a country area. A vicious potato blight had swept the county, and many local farmers were being ruined by it. One day a Christian farmer went out to his potato fields and discovered to his consternation that his whole crop was blighted. Wigglesworth was staying nearby and heard about it. He came out into the field and walked up and down the rows of potatoes for hours, casting out the blight in the name of Jesus, praying in faith that God would heal the crop. A few weeks later he learned that the Christian farmer's field was the only one in the district with healthy potatoes. He had a bumper, bountiful crop!

May God give us faith like Wigglesworth's today; may He give us some men and women of real faith. I wish that the weak, "according to thy will, O Lord" ministers and preachers of today would learn a lesson or two from this shocking man of faith! This is my prayer: "O God, save us from unbelieving pastors!"

God hates unbelief. He loves the sinner, but not his sin of unbelief. Scripture says, "See to it, brothers, that none of you has a sinful, unbelieving heart that turns away from the Living God" (Hebrews 3:12). The same passage also says that His people were not able to enter the Promised Land "because of their unbelief" (verse 19). Jesus often rebuked His followers for their lack of faith, and did so even after His resurrection (see Mark 16:14). He asked, "when the Son of Man comes, will he find faith on the earth?" (Luke 18:8).

Unbelief is the opposite of faith. It keeps multitudes out of the Kingdom, out of God's will, out of His salvation, out of His healing power. Everyone who ever went to hell went there because they did not believe. Unbelief dilutes the Gospel, compromises it and makes it a mere shadow of itself. The Danish philosopher Soren Kierkegaard said, "Christ turned water into wine . . . whereas the modern church has done something more difficult – it has turned wine into water!" The Church has lost the supernatural Resurrection Gospel and has replaced it with a human, social, wishey-washey, feeble message that is powerless!

65. Miracles at Home and Abroad

Wigglesworth used to lead a yearly convention at Preston in Lancashire. One year an elder from Newton Heath Church in Manchester became ill with rheumatic fever shortly before the convention. His friends from the church wrapped him up in a thick blanket and loaded him and his luggage onto the coach which was to take them all to Preston. The driver wasn't very happy about this, and remarked pointedly that his vehicle was a coach, not an ambulance! Once they were at the convention Wigglesworth laid hands on the sick man. The power of God came upon him and he was instantly healed! He changed out of his bedclothes into his suit and enjoyed the rest of the convention. The same coach driver took them all home again afterwards, and was astonished to see that the man who had been seriously ill was now completely well.

Another year a group of teenagers from the same church went to Preston on bicycles, since they couldn't afford to go by train or coach. As they descended the very steep hill into Preston, one of the lads discovered to his alarm that his brakes weren't working. He had put the brake blocks on the wrong way round! He had no way of stopping and ran right into a brick wall at the bottom of the hill. His head was badly bruised and began to swell ominously. The other lads got him safely to the convention and there put a wet towel around his head. By now it was very badly swollen. A few minutes later Wigglesworth arrived and laid hands on the lad. Very quickly the swelling disappeared and his head went back to its normal size.

At a later convention Wigglesworth prayed for a man who had just had both his ear drums removed at the local hospital. Wigglesworth informed him that he now had two new ear drums and told him to go to the hospital to have this verified. The surgeon who had removed the two diseased ear drums was utterly amazed to find that they had somehow been replaced! The man returned to Wigglesworth later that day, since his hearing was still not restored. Wigglesworth touched his ears, and then the man could hear again. He was even able to hear a woman's wristwatch ticking several feet away.

That same year Wigglesworth prayed for a man who had cancer of the throat. He told him to go home and have a good supper in the name of the Lord Jesus! As they left the meeting his wife protested, "How is he supposed to eat a good supper when his throat is so cancerous that he can't even swallow?" Nevertheless, on their way home the man bought a meal from a chip shop, and as he began to eat it at home he found that he could swallow perfectly. He enjoyed his meal! When he was examined in the morning there was found to be no trace of throat cancer. Praise the Lord!

One Friday night a man came to see Wigglesworth at his home. He had cancer in his right leg. Wigglesworth went upstairs to pray and after twenty minutes came down and told the man to go home and fast for three days and nights, drinking only water. The man did this and found that after three days his leg was completely healed and normal. He was a market gardener by profession, so as a token of his gratitude to God and to Wigglesworth he sent the preacher a crate full of beautiful tomatoes.

On one occasion Wigglesworth was sitting with a friend on a park bench. A policeman happened to walk past them, limping. Wigglesworth asked him what the trouble was, and the policeman answered that he had a verruca. Wigglesworth told him to take off his shoe and sock and put his foot on the bench. The policeman was a little taken aback by this but did as he was told. "I can't see any verruca there," said Wigglesworth. The astonished policeman looked for it but could find no trace of it. Wigglesworth told him, "Before you took your shoe and sock off the Lord told me that you had been healed." The delighted policeman was now able to walk without pain. Quite a few people gathered round to see what was going on. Wigglesworth explained and took the opportunity to give them a brief word about faith.

Wigglesworth was once on his way to Australia. The ship had passed through the Suez Canal and had reached Ceylon (now called Sri Lanka). Wigglesworth had been booked to conduct an evening meeting there while the ship was docked for a few hours. Many miracles were seen at the meeting. After he had returned to the ship a man who had gone into the town to do some shopping was carried back on board, having been bitten by a poisonous snake. He had become very weak and pale. The doctor shook his head as the man's heart slowed. He was slipping into unconsciousness. There was nothing that could be done for him. But then Wigglesworth laid hands on him and prayed for him. The onlookers were astonished when seconds later they saw the poison ooze out of the wound and trickle down the man's arm! After a few minutes the man's colour returned and he awoke. He got up from the sofa on which he had been laid and asked, "What are you all staring at?" He was fit and well within the hour!

News of this swept through the ship and into the town. Soon there were hundreds of folk on the quayside asking for healing. The ship was now due to set sail, but the captain told Wigglesworth that he was willing to wait for an hour. So he went down onto the quayside, where a multitude of diseased, broken, paralysed, pain-riddled people awaited him. He went among them and prayed for them. Scores of them were healed. Some of them were made well just by being touched by his shadow as he walked past. God did many miracles that day.

66. Only Human

Sometimes Wigglesworth would lapse into momentary depression. He was human, after all. When faced with some Christian's doubts or failure to act in faith, or when he didn't receive immediate answers to prayer, or when he faced a tough challenge, he would emit a deep sigh from his inmost being. Sometimes he was depressed by other Christians' opposition to his ministry. Often they would oppose him because they were oversensitive or unable to understand his unusually close walk with God. Also, he was ahead of his time and left many of his fellow preachers and pastors a million miles behind him! And, of course, there were those who were simply jealous of the success of his ministry, and there were those who were guilty of downright unbelief.

He was a very practical, straightforward, no-nonsense character. In fact he could be somewhat blunt at times. A Christian named Bob Fish had promised to meet him one day at Victoria Station in Manchester. He made it there before the train was due to arrive, but he was surprised to find that Wigglesworth was already on the platform, fuming irritably!

"You're an hour late, brother!" said the preacher. "I have been waiting on this draughty platform for a whole hour!"

"But brother Wigglesworth," protested Bob, "I have your letter here in my hand." He brandished the note he had received a few days earlier. "You said I was to meet you at 11.30 a.m., and that's the time now! You must have got the train's time of arrival wrong!"

Wigglesworth didn't reply but made his way with Bob out of the station, tut-tutting all the way. They took a taxi to Bob's house, and when they got there Wigglesworth told the driver off for overcharging!

As they got out of the taxi a woman was sweeping the pavement outside her house. Wigglesworth forgot all about his annoyance, laid hands on the woman and prayed, "Save this woman's soul, Lord! Make her strong for you! Amen!" The woman stopped in her tracks with sheer amazement. Quite overcome, she burst into tears and ran into her house. Soon afterwards she became a strong believer and followed the Lord to her dying day!

Once they were in Bob's home Mrs Fish asked Wigglesworth how he was. "Oh, I'm all right," he answered. "But I did get in rather early, and I put Bob out a bit." That was all he ever had to say on the subject, and Bob knew that it was his way of apologising. He was a great man of faith, but he made mistakes sometimes. When he did he knew how to climb down, how to be humble.

He was the chairman of the great yearly convention at Preston, which drew up to 1,500 people in its heyday. One year the famous Bible teacher Donald Gee was due to speak at it, but he had mistakenly double-booked and so was expected at the Leyland convention at the same time. When Wigglesworth heard about this he remonstrated with Gee in a very frank manner. "You knew you were booked here," he said. "What are you doing running off to other meetings when you had arranged to be here with us? *This is not good enough!*" The argument was quite heated, especially on Wigglesworth's side. Gee was quite dumbfounded, and eventually Wigglesworth fell silent too. Then Gee agreed that he had made a foolish mistake and that he should have been more careful with his bookings. He said he would cancel the Leyland meetings and would preach at Preston. Wigglesworth said no more, but then suddenly laid his hands on Gee's head and prayed, "Lord, give this man a better memory . . . and bless him as he goes to minister your Word to hungry souls at Leyland!" So it was Preston's loss but Leyland's gain. Wigglesworth, despite all his heated arguing, had stepped down. It was not the first time he had done that, and it would not be the last. Humility and modesty were two of his hallmarks, despite his tendency to bluntness and temper.

Wigglesworth spent quite a long time working in Norway. There he preached in a large park, where great numbers of people were prayed for and healed. This caused much consternation among the medical profession, who proposed a new law outlawing the laying on of hands. The preacher was invited to dine with the King and Queen. They wanted to meet Wigglesworth and see what kind of a man he was, since they would have to decide whether or not to consent to the bill. At that dinner Wigglesworth assured the Home Secretary, who was also present, that he need not bother to make the bill law, since from that time on he would not lay hands on anybody in Norway. And so at the next big meeting in the park Wigglesworth told the people to lay hands on themselves and prayed for them collectively. This so pleased the King that from then on Wigglesworth enjoyed considerable royal patronage and was able to preach the Full Gospel freely while he was in the country. This is all the more remarkable when one considers the fact that Wigglesworth was a simple, uneducated man. Through God's grace he not only failed to offend the King and Queen with his lack of polished table manners but, more than that, won them over to the cause of the Gospel.

Wigglesworth once stayed for a while at Houghbury Hall, the Bedfordshire home of a very wealthy man named Cecil Polhill. He was very impressed by Wigglesworth and his minsitry. One Saturday morning he asked the preacher to come with him into the grounds of the house. Polhill led him to a bench there and explained to him that this was a special bench, since it was his custom to present a cheque to anyone he brought there. He then gave the preacher a cheque for £100,000 (now worth about £3 million)! Wigglesworth was at first quite taken aback by this, but expressed his sincere gratitude. But then he felt he had to refuse to accept the cheque because he believed that such a large sum would make him covetous!

67. Taking Possession of the Land

When praying for a miracle or commencing some faith-testing project Wigglesworth would often start by praising God, since he knew that this was part of the secret of spiritual victory. He really believed in magnifying God and shouting His praises. On one occasion he was travelling to the USA, and the ship he was on wasn't making very good time. On the last day of the voyage Wigglesworth asked the captain when he expected to reach New York, since he was due to speak at a meeting in the city at 8.30 that evening.

"I'm afraid we have lost so much time that we're going to be late," confessed the captain.

So Wigglesworth began to praise God, there and then, in front of the embarassed but awe-stricken captain. "God is never late!" declared the man of faith. "He will not let his servants be late. We shall arrive at New York at 7.00 p.m., captain!"

Soon the ship somehow started to pick up speed. It got to New York harbour at 7.00! Wigglesworth had plenty of time to get through customs and make it to his meeting. "I nearly broke the speed record for crossing the Atlantic!" declared the captain afterwards. "I ought to have that preacher on board regularly – he's got greater power than the *Queen Mary*!" (She was the fastest ship in the world at that time.)

We can see from the life of Smith Wigglesworth that faith achieves what is in human terms downright impossible. It conquers the territory of man and the devil. God said to the children of Israel, "See, I have given you this land. Go in and take possession of the land" (Deuteronomy 1:8). We, in these modern times, also have a land to take for the glory of God. We are a new Joshua generation. We are the ones who are going to go over the Jordan and conquer the land. We are the ones who are going to pull down Jericho. We are going to do it – we are not going to fall. We are going to stand by faith.

But are God's people ready for this great challenge? There are too many Christians who are tired of pressing in to the things of God. They prefer to be like the world. But we are "a chosen people, a royal priesthood, a holy nation, a people belonging to God, that [we] may declare the praises of him who called [us] out of darkness into his wonderful light" (1 Peter 2:9). We are called to be different. We should walk and talk with integrity. We should have the praises of God on our lips. We should be thankful, we should be joyful. We should be full of faith. We should never surrender to circumstances. We should be full of peace. It grieves me to see Christian young people trying to be like the world. The world has nothing to offer.

If we, the Church, fail to rise to the challenge

of taking this nation for God, it will be because of *unbelief* and nothing else. It is unbelief that keeps us in a state of defeat, poverty and confusion. Satan would like to keep us in unbelief for as long as he can. He wants us to think that God cannot use us, that we are not ready yet. But let's not be unbelieving. In faith, in the name of Jesus, let us go in and possess the land that belongs to us!

It will be faith that will take us in. Faith in God will bring victory, healing and revival to this nation. I am believing God that His Kingdom will take over this land and the whole of Europe; I am believing God for a special move of the Holy Spirit. By faith we will take every school and university for Jesus; we will take the mass media too.

Hebrews chapter 11 tells us that by faith our spiritual forefathers administered justice, conquered kingdoms, received promises from God, shut the mouths of lions, stopped sin in their generations, won battles in their times and defeated their enemies. Their faith made them mighty. The faith that made them powerful in battle and strong in weakness is also the faith that lives in us today.

Let us not fall into the same trap that Israel fell into – the trap of unbelief. Act on the word, "Go in and possess the land" and you will see a mighty miracle in your church or in your ministry. Move in and possess the land, the victory, the miracle, the finance, the growth, the breakthrough, the revival – move in and possess what belongs to you. This is not optional. It is a *command*.

Go in and possess the best that God has in mind for you.

Go in and possess true spiritual worship. Take possession of dimensions of praise that you have never entered into before. Don't let the worship in your church get stale. Let us possess the signs and miracles that belong to us; let us press through and possess a new joy in God, a new dimension of peace, authority, victory, unity and evangelism. Let us become indwelt by God's presence. Let us not quench the Holy Spirit by refusing to lift our heads, open our hearts and raise our voices in praise and worship.

Also, let us not grieve the Spirit with unconfessed sin in our lives. God has made it possible for us to walk in total victory over all known sin. The place of victory is a place of repentance and forgiveness, of quiet rest, close to the heart of God. We must walk the victory walk!

The Church of God in this country is no longer a sleeping child. God has been moulding, breaking and preparing us, and now we are ready. The fear of God is upon the land – the heathen will tremble before the move of God and the authority of His people.

He has showed us in his Word how to possess the land: "Set out now and cross the Arnon gorge. See, I have given into your hand Sihon the Amorite, king of Heshbon, and his country. Begin to take possession of it and engage him in battle. This very day I will put the terror and fear of you on all the nations under heaven" (Deuteronomy 2:24-25).

Smith Wigglesworth, whose legacy and mantle come down on us in this present generation sixty years after his heyday of power, was such a one, who moved in the might, authority and fear of our all-powerful God. He was walking in Essex one day when a man passed him by on the pavement, Smith stopped his conversation with the Pastor, suddenly grabbed this man and threw him down on to an allotment alongside the path. He held the man down in the cabbages, and praying declared: "You are a backslider, but you will return to the Saviour and bring forth much fruit". He let the man go as suddenly as he had seized him, lying there in the garden!

As they walked on, the pastor, somewhat perturbed, enquired if he knew the man, and Smith replied that he had never seen him before!

A year later the evangelist was back in that county, and was thrilled to see the gospel hall he was to preach at densely packed well before the meeting. He asked the elder how it was so, because last time he spoke there, only a handful had turned up. BUT THE PLACE WAS ALIVE! The elder replied, "It was through you, Wigglesworth. See that man over there (pointing to the same fellow he had dealt with in the cabbages) God set him on fire, AND HE HAS WON ALL THESE FOLK IN THIS SERVICE . . ."! FAITH, FEARLESS-NESS, DARING is rewarded.

I challenge you to be a confronter and a conqueror.

68. Revolutionary Christians

We Christans need to be revolutionaries — we must pray and work to transform the society in which we live. By the power of God we can radically improve the spiritual climate of the whole country. The words of the prophet apply to us today: "Arise, shine, for your light has come, and the glory of the Lord rises upon you" (Isaiah 60:1). Yes, there is darkness in this land, but there is also the light of the Lord, which forces the darkness to flee. We must spread that light throughout this nation.

The people of this land are hurting and in confusion. They are waiting to hear from God. The harvest is plentiful. However, the labourers are few. We need to get out into the fields and gather the harvest.

We need to be militant Christians. We must stand up as the army of God — an army anointed by Him to do His will.

We must be living and working in time with God's heartbeat. We must ask ourselves what He wants us to do with our lives. We should be constantly seeking fresh anointing and direction from Him so that we may win souls for Him.

We must represent the Lord Jesus. We mustn't just

"talk the talk"; we must "walk the walk" – we must live to glorify God. This nation's future depends on us humbling ourselves, praying, fulfilling God's will and becoming His ambassadors and anointed ministers.

We need to be open to God and to let Him expose everything in our lives which is not of Him, so that we can do the things that are of Him. For example, those of us involved in the ministry may be tempted to think too highly of ourselves. Or when Christians pray for the sick, their motives may be wrong, and so they do not see results every time. Why do we pray for the sick? Because we want to glorify ourselves? We should pray out of genuine love for the suffering and out of a desire to glorify God.

Never has there been an hour like this one! There has never been a more crucial time, there has never been a greater need for the people of God *to show their faith, to act out their faith, to do exploits, to work miracles!* Ingersoll, the notable atheist, said, "Show me the signs and wonders and miracles of the Bible and I will believe in Christianity." That is the challenge to which we must rise. The world is waiting to see the power of God.

When faith makes demands upon the written Word of God, that Word comes alive. Jesus said, "The words I have spoken to you are Spirit and they are life" (John 6:63). No word of God is void of power; every word God speaks contains in itself the power for its own fulfilment. God has given us living words which heal, bless, save, prosper and change human nature. We must accept the absolute lordship of God's Book over our lives. Through faith, we can bring about a spiritual revolution in Britain, in Europe and across the world.

As Charles Wesley wrote: "Inspire the living faith, the faith that conquers all." *Faith*, Hebrews 2:6, GNB, tells us, "Is being sure of what we hope for." Its guide book is the Bible, and the marks of a true man or woman of faith is a well-fed soul, a well-read Bible. "The book of the law shall not depart from your mouth . . . day (or) night."

Mavis, twenty-three years paralysed, thirteen long years in a wheelchair, bound, sad, sick, suddenly is set free, A MIRACLE! She walks from one of my services, and is still free two years later, a testimony to hundreds of thousands of unsaved people in Yorkshire. Faith moves the hand of God TODAY.

Wigglesworth said: "WE MUST GET RID OF OUR SMALL MEASURE OF FAITH". GOD HONOURS FAITH – FAITH HONOURS GOD. Watching a little squirrel recently, bravely taking huge leaps across a tree, from one high branch to another, tells us that to win – WE MUST RISK, take the leap of faith into God's sure hands. REVIVAL IS IN THE AIR, the Spirit of faith is released in our land, I am seeing literally thousands Born Again and miraculously healed, HEAVEN IS ON OUR SIDE, God is upon us in an AWESOME WAY. "NOTHING LIKE THIS HAS EVER BEEN SEEN IN OUR LAND BEFORE. . . ." (Matthew 9:33). BIBLE DAYS ARE HERE AGAIN! REVIVAL BREAKTHROUGH AND A RE-BIRTH OF FAITH IS ON THE WAY!

Radiant
Christian Living

The Rev. Melvin Banks has held vibrant, exciting, successful evangelistic and divine healing missions for thirty years across the UK and in twenty-five nations of the world, bringing the Gospel to hundreds of thousands of unchurched people. This year alone he will preach in a hundred different areas of the country and in nine other nations.

He loves to hear from ministers, churches and individuals. Anyone can write to him (please send S.A.E.) for prayer, advice and free literature.

Write to:

THE REV. MELVIN BANKS
CRUSADE OFFICE
44 MONKS WAY
CHIPPENHAM, WILTS
SN15 3TT, ENGLAND